Heroes and Other Mortals

Heroes and Other Mortals
Stories of Our Better Angels

Frye Gaillard

NewSouth Books
an imprint of
The University of Georgia Press
Athens

NSB

Published by NewSouth Books,
an imprint of the University of Georgia Press
Athens, Georgia 30602
https://ugapress.org/imprints/newsouth-books/

© 2025 by Frye Gaillard
Foreword © 2025 by Cynthia Tucker
All rights reserved
Designed by Mary McKeon
Illustration by Candice Fairchild
Set in 10/13 Adobe Caslon Pro by Mary McKeon

Printed and bound by Sheridan Books, Inc.
The paper in this book meets the guidelines for
permanence and durability of the Committee on
Production Guidelines for Book Longevity of the
Council on Library Resources.

Most NewSouth/University of Georgia Press titles are
available from popular e-book vendors.

Printed in the United States of America
25 26 27 28 29 P 5 4 3 2 1

Library of Congress Cataloging-in-Publication Data
Names: Gaillard, Frye, 1946– author.
Title: Heroes and other mortals : stories of our better angels / Frye Gaillard.
Other titles: Stories of our better angels
Description: Athens : NewSouth Books, an imprint of the University of Georgia Press, [2025]
Identifiers: LCCN 2024034299 | ISBN 9781588385444 (paperback) | ISBN 9781588385451 (epub) | ISBN 9781588385468 (pdf)
Subjects: LCSH: Biography. | Civilization, Modern—1950–
Classification: LCC CT101 .G35 20 | DDC 909.82/50922—dc23/eng/20241205
LC record available at https://lccn.loc.gov/2024034299

These stories originally appeared, sometimes in different form, via the following venues: *Alabama Heritage*, the *Alabama Review*, Alabama Writers Forum, the *Americana Gazette*, the *Bitter Southerner*, *Chapter 16*, the *Charlotte Observer*, Facebook, the *Guardian*, the *Journal of American History*, *Mobile Bay Magazine*, Mobile Museum of History, the *Mobile Press Register*, NewSouth Books, the *Oracle*, Oxford University Press, *Race Relations Reporter*, *Salvation South*, The University of Georgia Press, *United Methodist News*, the *Vanderbilt Hustler*, and *Vanderbilt Magazine*.

To the memory of Nancy Gaillard and the legacy of Rosalynn and
Jimmy Carter, all of whom, in remarkable ways,
embodied what this book is about

I have seen the Promised Land . . . I may not get there with you . . .
—Dr. Martin Luther King Jr.

I can feel the suffering of millions and yet, if I look up into the heavens, I think that it will all come right.
—Anne Frank

CONTENTS

Foreword, by Cynthia Tucker	ix
Introduction	1
The Broken Road of Peggy Wallace Kennedy (2020)	5
The Rabbi and Dr. King (2020)	17
Bishop Tutu: "The Blasphemy of Apartheid" (1986)	26
A Prophetic Journalist (1985)	30
Mikhail Gorbachev: "A Man of Peace" (1990)	37
Shaking Hands with Jane Goodall (2023)	46
The Bayou Doctor (2008)	57
Songs of the South	
Coal: The West Virginia Roots of a Country Star (2012)	70
The Dreaming Fields of Matraca Berg (2011)	77
715: A Baseball Legend in a Country Song (2009)	82
Reclaiming the Legacy of a Country Music Star (2023)	86
The Chancellor (2009)	89
Madness: The Agony and Triumph of Elyn Saks (2011)	92
Helen Keller: Monument to a Radical Idealist (2022)	100
Little School on a Hill (2021)	104
The Odyssey of Chief Calvin McGhee (2021)	108
The Slave Who Went to Congress (2013)	115
The Story of a Typewriter (2020)	124
Books That Matter	
The Last Slave Ship (2022)	128

Fugitives of the Heart (2021)	132
Atticus Finch: The Biography (2020)	135
Sidney Poitier: "We'll Catch a Later Plane" (2023)	139
"Thank God, a Young Person Had a Camera" (2023)	142
The Southernization of America (2022)	154
Keeper of the Faith (2022)	161
Musings: Commencement 2018	163
Acknowledgments	*167*
About the Author	*168*

FOREWORD

Frye Gaillard is a talented storyteller—poetic, empathetic, prolific, and, most important, wise. He launched his journalism career in 1970, at the end of a tumultuous decade characterized by political assassinations, racial strife, police brutality, and government-sanctioned violence but also by the power and possibility of the civil rights movement. Ever the optimist, Frye has focused on redemptive possibility, telling the stories of people who have struck a blow for justice, for liberation, for equality.

He didn't set out to write those stories. Like many journalists of his time and place (myself included), he believed that journalism was a way to change the world. He believed that if he used the power of his pen to expose injustice, uncover oppression, and unmask racism, sexism, homophobia, and other forms of bigotry, politicians and their allies would do the right thing.

Alas, he discovered (as did I) that changing the world is not quite so simple as that. The status quo is powerful, as are the reactionary forces that resist social change. Still, Frye frequently found himself investigating and interrogating the lives of people who were committed to a more just and more compassionate world. In a long and prestigious career, he has written about people both famous and obscure—politicians, artists, academics, activists, common folk—but all with one thing in common: they stood up for a righteous cause, perhaps through a lifetime of committed activism, perhaps through a few moments of courageous action.

The narratives included here are wide ranging. Frye writes about well-known figures such as Mikhail Gorbachev, Bishop Tutu, and Jane Goodall, but, as a son of the South, he is especially interested in native Southerners who stood on the right side of history.

Again, those include well-known figures such as Helen Keller, but also lesser-known people such as Peggy Wallace Kennedy, the daughter of George Wallace. She has spent decades working to narrow the racial chasms her father helped to widen. Frye also writes about the storm-battered Gulf Coast village of Bayou La Batre and its hardworking, down-to-earth physician, Dr. Regina Benjamin, who was later appointed by President Obama to be U.S. surgeon general. He writes about singer-songwriter Kathy Mattea, who left a lucrative country music career to capture the beauty and tragedy of her native Appalachia in folk music.

As disparate as the narratives in this collection are, there is a thread that connects them: they all feature people willing to forge a path toward a more hopeful and compassionate world. These stories are a balm for our troubled times.

Cynthia Tucker, University of South Alabama
journalist in residence, winner of the Pulitzer Prize

Heroes and Other Mortals

INTRODUCTION

In 1970, I set out on career as a writer, filled with hope and misconception about the fundamental nature of the craft. I was a journalist, a child of the sixties, certain that the power of the truth could set us free, could guide us in the quest to right old wrongs and make the world more just. For a while, that seemed to be the case. Early in my career, I was a staff writer at the *Race Relations Reporter*, a small publication funded by the Ford Foundation, where I was surrounded by distinguished mentors, and embarked, I thought, on a noble mission. We were charged with trying to understand the racial struggles taking place in America.

I was assigned to the Indian beat. These were the days when Native American activists had seized control of an abandoned prison on Alcatraz Island. They arrived in a fleet of small boats, shrouded by the mists of San Francisco Bay, and in the dampness of a California night, scaled a crumbling stairway up the slopes of the Rock—the name given by prisoners to this terrible place of incarceration.

Here they proclaimed a reversal of history. For centuries the U.S. government had seized native land; now the Indians were taking it back. To try to understand what was happening, I called a writer named Vine Deloria Jr., a Standing Rock Sioux from North Dakota, who would become, unexpectedly, a mentor and friend. In 1969, Deloria had written *Custer Died for Your Sins: An Indian Manifesto*, chastising white America for its centuries of genocidal abuse.

We talked about the Alcatraz protests—a fine thing, he thought, but mostly symbolic. He pointed me toward more tangible disputes, a struggle in Washington State, for example, by the Quinalts and other tribes to reclaim the unfettered right to fish, just as their ancestors had always done; or the quest by leaders of the Yakima Nation to get their mountain back.

I wrote about both of those issues, but especially the Yakimas, who lived at the base of Mount Adams, part of that stunningly beautiful chain of volcanoes, thought to be dormant until, a few years later, the massive eruption of Mount Saint Helens. To the Yakimas, Mount Adams was sacred. It was easy enough to understand why, for it rose from the valley floor to a height of 12,500 feet. It was permanently snowcapped, towering far above the evergreen forests, and occupied a majestic place in the cosmology of the tribe. The Yakimas' treaty was clear. The eastern face of the mountain, the one looking out across the reservation, belonged unambiguously to the Indians.

For a century, the U.S. government had denied that claim. In 1970, I began to write about that injustice, as did a couple of other journalists, most notably William Greider of the *Washington Post*. Soon, a curious thing began to happen. The Nixon administration grew embarrassed, a contrast to the lack of bureaucratic shame that had prevailed for the past hundred years. For one thing, the issue was so clear-cut. It was impossible to argue that government surveyors in the 1860s had failed in good faith to notice the mountain or to continue to justify their mistake. Beyond that, Nixon officials, who were then under fire for retreating from civil rights legislation, were eager to tout their sympathy for Native Americans. For whatever reason, President Nixon on May 20, 1972, issued an executive order affirming the Yakimas' claim to the mountain.

For a twenty-five-year-old reporter, it was a moment both heady and humbling when tribal leaders invited me to the Yakimas' celebration. They presented me with a handmade belt, crafted by one of the elders. I still cherish it, of course. But I no longer see it, as I did back then, as a symbol of the power of the pen. For one thing, almost nothing of the same sort has ever happened again, and fully a half century has passed. Yes, it is true that the work of a journalist can become part of the public dialogue, can even help to give it a shape. Later in the 1970s, I covered the school busing crisis in Charlotte, North Carolina, and later turned that coverage into a book, *The Dream Long Deferred*, guided by the admonitions of my editor, Jim Batten, at the *Charlotte Observer*.

"Your job," he told me, "is not to tell this community what to think. It is to provide enough information so that it *can* think as it confronts its most serious social crisis in fifty years."

As a community, Charlotte soon earned a national reputation for its successful desegregation of schools. I would like to think that the *Observer*'s coverage was a factor. All reporters—all of us who write with an eye toward history and truth—hope that about their work. But for me at least, the moments of measurable results are so exceedingly rare as to be an aberration.

James Baldwin, one of the great writers of the twentieth century, used to say that his life's work was simply bearing witness. He regarded this as a lesser calling than others he could name:

> I did not have to deal with the criminal state of Mississippi hour by hour and day by day, to say nothing of night after night. I did not have to sweat cold sweat after decisions involving hundreds of thousands of lives. I was not responsible for raising money or deciding how to use it. I was not responsible for strategy, controlling prayer meetings, marches, petitions, voting registration drives. I saw the sheriffs, the deputies, the storm troopers, more or less in passing. I was never in town to stay. This was sometimes hard on my morale . . . but I had to accept as time wore on, that part of my responsibility as a witness was to move as largely and as freely as possible. To write the story and get it out.

The story he wrote broke his heart. "It comes as a great shock," he said, "to discover the country which is your birthplace, and to which you owe your life and identity has not—in its whole system of reality—evolved any place for you." That was, in a sense, his epitaph for America even as he tried to hold on to hope. And most of us understood what he meant. Indeed, I would say that for my generation, coming of age in the 1960s, the past half century has been mostly a trajectory of heartache.

We had such hopes back in the days of once upon a time . . . when four college freshmen in Greensboro, North Carolina, gave new life to the civil rights movement with the simple act of sitting in at a lunch counter, when a handsome young president helped us believe in New Frontiers, and Dr. Martin Luther King Jr. delivered his sermon on the Washington mall about the possibilities of brotherhood and justice. But then came wars of choice and assassinations and the massive cynicism of politicians, culminating in 2016 with the election of a president so toxic that we reel even now over what it says about us. Our democracy, we find, hangs in the balance in a violent land.

A writer, understanding by now the limits of his craft, bears witness to all of this. How could he not?

But I have discovered a curious thing, and I'm still not sure what to make of it. Perhaps as a matter of self-defense, I have tended to write about hard truth by celebrating people who make things better. Or at least who try. This was not a deliberate choice so much as a recurring theme that I became aware of only later. Some of the people whose stories I have told set out consciously to change the world, often in the grandest of ways. Others simply did what they do. But all of them were women and men whose stories seemed to me to be important . . . a doctor, two lawyers, and an Indian chief; a rabbi, three Nobel Peace Prize winners, and a member of Congress; a baseball legend and a handful of writers, some country music stars, and one of the greatest scientists of our time.

Some of them succeeded in what they were trying to do. Others did not. But with gratitude, I have collected a few of their stories here. I am honored by that opportunity. I hope there is inspiration in the telling, for where would the rest of us be without them?

Frye Gaillard, 2023

The Broken Road of Peggy Wallace Kennedy

> This article first appeared in the *Bitter Southerner*, which has published some of the finest writers in the South. On several occasions, I've been honored to have my words among them.

It was a day in early spring, the faint chill of winter still in the air, when Peggy Wallace Kennedy and her husband Mark stopped at the grave of Martin Luther King. Their young son, Burns, who was eight or nine, trailed along behind them, and the family was on a journey of reconciliation. Peggy is the daughter of Governor George C. Wallace, and on this day in 1996, in what she knew were the closing years of his life, she was trying to come to terms with his legacy.

She had never fully shared his views on race, not when he stood in the schoolhouse door, or when he declared a few days before the Birmingham church bombing that the nation needed "a few first-class funerals." Peggy loved her father, more in fact as time went by, but she also knew he was a difficult man, who had done grave harm to the South and the country. As Dr. King once told him in a telegram, "The blood of our children is on your hands." Peggy understood that this was so.

"As I grew older," she says, "I realized my father had created a climate with his words and actions that made other people go out and do horrible things. That was very hard to take."

Thus did she and Mark and their son stand together at the grave of Dr. King, and reflect on the heritage of their family and place. They knew that King had begun his career—his remarkably brief moment on the stage of history—at the Dexter Avenue Baptist Church in Montgomery. It is one of the visual ironies of the civil rights years that the little brick chapel, completed in 1889, stands barely a stone's throw down a hill from the gleaming marble of the Alabama Capitol—the edifice from which George Wallace once promised, "Segregation now, segregation tomorrow, segregation forever!"

In the family's pilgrimage into that history, they absorbed the quiet at the King gravesite, the reverential whispers among the tourists who had gathered, then walked together up a residential street—"like any other," Mark remembered—to the house where Dr. King had lived. As they wandered through the rooms, the parents could see in the eyes of their son that Martin Luther King was becoming more real, no longer a statue or stick figure from the past but a man with a family who had lived in this place, and who had died—they could see this from the dates on the grave—when he was only thirty-nine years old.

Then came the museum. It was a newly constructed memorial to the work of Dr. King and the turbulence and progress of the civil rights years. As they rounded a corner, they came to an exhibit—a story told in large photographs—of an ugly time in the Heart of Dixie. There was George Wallace in the schoolhouse door, and there were the dogs and fire hoses in Birmingham, and the rubble of the Sixteenth Street Baptist Church, where four young girls barely older than Burns had been killed by a bomb. And finally, there were images from the Edmund Pettus Bridge: Alabama State Troopers, ordered by Wallace to stop a march from Selma to Montgomery, beating demonstrators senseless in a cloud of tear gas.

After a long and somber silence, Burns looked up at his mother and asked, "Why did Paw Paw do those things to other people?"

More than twenty years later, Peggy grew emotional when she told that story. "It was the question," she said, "that changed my life, I thought to myself, 'I've got to do for Burns what my father never did for me.' I drew him close and said, 'Paw Paw never told me why he did those things. Maybe we will have to make it right."

In the years since then Peggy has tried. Slowly and quietly she has emerged as an advocate of peace and reconciliation, and now in the shadow of another troubled time, she has published a memoir about her experience. The book, written in collaboration with Mark, is called *The Broken Road: George Wallace and a Daughter's Journey to Reconciliation*. As the title suggests, this is really two stories in one. It is Peggy's first of all, and her struggle to overcome the sins of the past is a familiar journey to many white Southerners. If we are honest, most of us have been there, but we also see, as we read these pages, that few people feel the burden more keenly than the daughter of George Wallace.

That is the second story in her book—her father's—and in her telling, Wallace is a gifted politician, who left a legacy of racism and rage, and knew that he had done it, and desperately, urgently sought to make amends. This is a daughter's portrait of a man who led three public lives, who fashioned, in a sense, three political careers. Two of those—the first and the last—were defined by decency as well as ambition. But the one in the middle, the one for which he will be remembered, stoked the fires of division and hate. And through it all there was the specter of pain. That is where the Wallace story begins. The redemption Peggy offers in *The Broken Road* is the hope that pain is not where it will end.

He spent a troubled boyhood in Clio, Alabama, a town described by journalist Theodore White as a "seedy, mournful village" where the people found respite from the drudgeries of life in gossip about politics and race. In this desultory place, when others his age might dream of being a cowboy, or perhaps a fireman or baseball star, George Wallace dreamed of something different. He wanted to be governor of Alabama.

He came from the family of fading rural prominence. His grandfather, the first George Wallace, was a country doctor who often bartered for his service with small-town patients who could not pay. It was a modest patriarchy rooted in respect, though not in wealth, and respect would vanish in the next generation. By any measure, the second George Wallace, father of the future governor, was a source of misery for his family. Against the backdrop of the Great Depression, he was, as one of his sons remembered, "a man of indiscretion and perpetual drunkenness." In *The Broken Road,* Peggy offers this description of her father's childhood:

> When Daddy and his brothers, Gerald and Jack, were young boys, my grandfather would push the living room furniture up against the walls, roll up the rugs, and force the three boys to fight. The Clio telephone company was on the second floor of the building across the street and the operator could see right into Daddy's living room. On fight nights, the operator agreed to time the rounds and ring the Wallace phone when each was over. Sometimes she would ring the phone early when the fighting got out of hand. Most times that act of mercy didn't matter—a round was over when my grandfather said it was and not a moment sooner. On many nights the fight ended with my grandfather passed out

drunk on the floor. When that happened, his wife, Mozelle, covered him with a blanket while her sons went off to lick their wounds.

Almost certainly, the pain of such moments was multilayered, for in addition to a father's cruelty, and a mother's helpless inability to stop it, there was also the fact that everybody knew. A family once respected for the healer at its head was now the object of pity and disdain, the whispered gossip of a small Southern town. For the youngest George Wallace, politics—the great blood sport of the rural South—became his chosen path of escape. As a teenager serving as a legislative page, he stood erect on the star near the steps of the capitol, where Jefferson Davis had taken his oath, and dreamed of the day when he would do the same. "I knew then," he said later, "that I would be governor."

In the 1940s, during his early pursuit of that goal, he allied himself with the progressive wing of Alabama politics. It is one of the unexpected truths of history that Alabama, in those days, was home to some of the most liberal leaders in the South—men nationally respected in the Democratic Party. U.S. senator Lister Hill was dean of politics in the state, a man most remembered for his 1946 legislation, the Hill-Burton Act, to fund hospitals in rural America. As a senator with strong New Deal sensibilities, Hill supported increases in the minimum wage and federal funding of libraries and schools. His Senate protégé John Sparkman followed his lead, earning such admiration in the party that he was chosen in 1952 as the running mate for Adlai Stevenson.

But all of that changed with the issue of race—a reality from which Hill and Sparkman both retreated in a way that George Wallace did not. Not at first. Instinctively, as a young politician, he was drawn to Big Jim Folsom, one of Alabama's most colorful governors. Folsom was, in the words of journalist Ray Jenkins, "something of a closet integrationist." He once shared drinks in the governor's mansion with Adam Clayton Powell, a fearless advocate of civil rights, who represented Harlem in Congress. And when segregationists complained, as he knew they would, Folsom dismissed them as "hound dogs baying at the moon."

More substantially, he appointed registrars, particularly in Macon County and Mobile, who opened the rolls to thousands of Black voters. Though he was often accused of corruption, Folsom was a man who meant to make a difference. Wallace knew this and as a Folsom supporter he asked the governor to appoint him to the board of Tuskegee Institute, the college founded by Booker T. Washington. By all accounts Wallace served conscientiously, which was also true in the 1950s, when he was elected as an Alabama circuit judge.

"George Wallace," said J. L. Chestnut, a Black civil rights attorney from Selma, "was the most liberal judge I ever practiced in front of. He was the first judge in Alabama to call me 'Mister' in his courtroom."

Wallace brought those same sensibilities—the economic populism of the New Deal and a message of racial moderation—to his first run for governor in 1958. "He cared about things like roads and schools," his daughter remembered, "things that would actually make life better." As election day approached, Wallace stared at the camera in a TV ad, his dark eyes softer than they would seem later on, and declared with an evident sense of conviction: "I want to tell the good people of this state . . . if I didn't have what it took to treat a man fair regardless of the color of his skin, then I don't have what it takes to be the governor of your great state."

Wallace, however, faced a formidable opponent. John Patterson, the state's segregationist attorney general, made no promises about treating people fairly. Taking a stance he would later regret, Patterson drew a hard line on the issue of race. "Once you let the bar down," he proclaimed, "it's all over." He ran with support from the Ku Klux Klan, and told the voters he was "honored" to have it. He won in a landslide.

In *The Broken Road*, Peggy Kennedy writes of a sad election night with her family: "Daddy gathered us up and took us to a waiting car to drive to a local television station on the outskirts of Montgomery. He was going to concede. I sat in the middle of the front seat next to Daddy and buried my face in his side. I felt his arm surround me as he pulled me close and whispered: 'Well, we lost, Sugah, but it is going to be all right. Sweetie, now don't you cry.' The tears I was drying with the handkerchief he pulled from his pocket were not for me, they were for him."

She also wrote of the dark underside of that tender moment. A few days after his defeat, Wallace paid a visit to Seymore Trammell, the district attorney of Barbour County, Alabama, who had been one of the leaders in his campaign. "Seymore," he said, "I was outniggered by John Patterson, and I'll tell you here and now, I will never be outniggered again."

In a sense, in that ugly and fateful declaration, Wallace announced the end of his first career—an identity rooted in racial moderation—and embarked on a path of cynical ambition that would cause indelible harm. Certainly, it was true that his Faustian bargain became a source of pain for his family—especially a little girl who, then as later, always wanted so much to love him.

He had long been an absentee father, and in the four years that followed his first run for governor, all of that grew worse. Wallace brooded and raged, and disappeared from home for long periods of time. All his life he had dreamed of being governor, and now at the age of thirty-nine he faced the possibility that it might not happen. Desperate for attention, he began to spend most of his time in Montgomery, hanging out in restaurants, hotel lobbies, and bars—anywhere he might find a crowd. He was drinking again, sometimes heavily, and he became less discreet in the womanizing that had always enraged his wife, Lurleen. There were frequent fights when he did come home, during which she often threatened to leave him.

"What can you do, Lurleen?" Wallace would say. "You don't have any skills. You're not smart. Where are you going to go? How are you going to live?"

"He could be brutal," writes Peggy. "Hard as nails. I went numb inside when Daddy treated Mama that way."

Finally, Lurleen did leave. She packed up her children (Peggy was the second oldest of four) and moved to her parents' house outside of Tuscaloosa. It occurred to her then that there might be a way to make her husband change. Lurleen decided to file for divorce. This was Alabama in the 1950s, and divorce, she knew, would be a deal-breaker for too many voters. Wallace got the message. His brother Gerald, who admired Lurleen, warned him he better make things right, or "you will be a two-time loser and going to somebody else's inauguration come January of 1963."

Wallace did what he had to do.

When he ran for governor in 1962, with Lurleen now back at his side, he campaigned with a kind of bare-knuckled ferocity that would soon become his trademark. As Dan Carter wrote in his acclaimed biography, *The Politics of Rage*, Wallace understood the resentments that simmered in a state like his own—a place deeply scarred by its rural poverty, where the struggles of life could sometimes ennoble but just as often embitter. And buried somewhere near the heart of it all was the issue of race.

Pulitzer Prize–winning author Rick Bragg, who grew up hard in northern Alabama, remembered being a boy at a Wallace rally, too young to understand all of what was being said, but still being clear about the fundamental message: people like his family were better than the Blacks. "We had not known," Bragg wrote, "that we were better than anybody."

Peggy Kennedy wrote of such things too, and an almost frightening kind of excitement when her father won and took the oath of office. At the age of twelve, she was awestruck by the ceremony of inauguration day—and by the roaring approval that came from the crowd when Wallace, a superb Southern orator, delivered an address written for him by a Klansman: "In the name of the greatest people that have ever trod this earth, I draw the line in the dust and toss the gauntlet before the feet of tyranny, and I say segregation now, segregation tomorrow, segregation forever."

The story of the next ten years is all too familiar. Wallace stood in the schoolhouse door and unleashed a torrent of incendiary rhetoric that created a climate in which people died. These were the images that came to define him—a bombed-out church, police dogs tearing at a teenager's flesh, and always the jutting jaw and defiant words of the governor, stirring the racism that was always there. Peggy knew that this was true. She also knew that when her father ran for president in 1964 and 1968, he helped teach the nation to think in code. His campaign slogan, "Stand Up for America", really meant, she admitted, "stand up for white Southerners," or the white working class in the North and Midwest.

In a grim foreshadowing of a future time, she saw the violence at his campaign rallies. "In 1968," she said, "he had a lot of African American protesters who would fight with Wallace people. I remember people throwing chairs."

Wallace himself did little to discourage it. In June 1968, while railing against "anarchist demonstrators and hippies," he told an audience of his supporters in Memphis, "If you will elect me president and any anarchists lie down in front of my car that will be the last car they ever lie down in front of." This was the dark and brilliant heart of his charisma, to reach deep into the resentments of the crowd and stir them into a catharsis of hate—to make the people in his audience believe that their worst instincts were actually their best. It was a powerful tonic in America, and some would argue that it changed the political DNA of the country.

Then came 1972. On May 15, running for president yet again, he was shot at a campaign rally in Maryland. The bullet pierced his spine. Peggy, who was then in college, flew to Maryland and rushed to Holy Cross Hospital, where he had undergone life-saving surgery. There was an eerie unreality about the scene:

> A battery of surgical lights suspended from the ceiling over Daddy's bed cast beams of pure white. Humming machines with blinking red and

green lights and tubes sprouting from their bottoms and sides stood haphazardly about. I shivered in the cold. Armed Secret Service agents stood in the shadows. . . . "Hey, Daddy, this is Peggy," I said. "I came to see you as fast as I could." I began to cry. Daddy looked my way. "Now, sweetie, don't you cry. It's going to be all right."

In the coming hours, other visitors would make their way to his bedside. One of them was Ethel Kennedy, who, four years earlier, had lost her husband to an assassin. She said Robert Kennedy would want her to be there. Peggy was surprised and moved by the visit, but the most astonishing well-wisher of all was a woman who was also running for president. Shirley Chisholm was a fierce trailblazer, the first woman to seek the nomination of a major party, and the first Black woman elected to Congress. Among the ranks of her radical followers was a former Black Panther named Barbara Lee, a future member of Congress, who warned her sternly, "Don't you go visit that racist."

Chisholm brushed the warning aside.

During her short time in Congress, in addition to her militant pursuit of equality, Chisholm had established a counterreputation for reaching across the aisle, and working with people very different from herself. She collaborated with Senator Bob Dole, a Kansas Republican, to expand food stamps and create to create a nutrition program for women, infants, and children (WIC). Because of white allies, Chisholm said, "poor babies have milk and poor children have food." But now her spirit of generosity was being pushed to new and untested limits. George Wallace was a man who stood for things she found repugnant. And yet he was also a human being and as he lay badly wounded in a hospital bed, unable to move the lower parts of his body, she found it inside herself to reach out.

"She and daddy talked real low," remembered Peggy. "They prayed together. Daddy asked her, 'What are your people going to say about you being here?' She told him it didn't matter; 'I would not want this to happen to anyone.' Daddy's face changed. There was just something that came over him. I think a seed was planted that day."

Mark Kennedy, who later became close to his father-in-law—"as close as anybody could be to the governor"—thought Wallace had never been a man of empathy. But now in the visit with Shirley Chisholm, he had been its recipient in an unexpected way, and all he could do was lie there and think.

In the months and years that followed, Wallace talked to both Peggy and Mark about events of the 1960s, including the Birmingham church bombing, and how, in the unflinching words of his daughter, "his actions and rhetoric had caused four little girls to die." Sometimes he grew defensive, and his thoughts were a jumble of rationalization. In *The Broken Road*, Peggy writes of a conversation in which he declared, "I was never against the blacks. I never, in any of my speeches, made slanderous or derogatory comments about the blacks.... I resent the continuing branding of me as a racist.... The issue I felt so strongly about was the issue of the growing federal bureaucracy and how it would devastate the state's sovereign power."

But as he made his way through the bitterness that went with his wounds, his depression over life as a paraplegic, his introspections grew more honest. No, he was not just talking about states' rights, and yes he was sorry for his mistakes. In his later years, said Peggy in a recent interview, her father would talk for hours "about how wrong he was on race and segregation."

"I know that now," he told her. "I've had a lot of time to think about it."

Nor was this merely his private remorse. On a Sunday morning in 1979, Wallace made an unannounced visit to Dr. King's Dexter Avenue Baptist Church, where he told the congregation, "I have learned what suffering means. I think I can understand something of the pain black people have come to endure. I know I contributed to that pain and I can only ask for forgiveness."

Some observers in Alabama, including white journalists such as the late Bob Ingram, remained forever skeptical about Wallace's remorse. Many people, said Ingram, thought the governor was merely "auditioning for heaven," while others noted that he "knew how to count." African Americans, once denied the ballot, were now registered to vote in large numbers, and in his final run for governor, Wallace overwhelmingly won their vote. As Peggy acknowledged in *The Broken Road*, he paid that political debt in full:

> During his last term of office, beginning in 1983, Daddy would appoint 160 African American Alabamians to state boards and agencies and double the number of black voter registrars in Alabama's sixty-seven counties.... He had done what he could to disenfranchise and even destroy the black community, and Daddy believed God struck him down for what he had done. He began to come to terms with the suffering he had

caused others. There was a connection in his mind between his journey to redemption through suffering and African Americans' journey to freedom through suffering.

That is the larger truth Peggy holds in her heart, and offers in the pages of her book: the change in George Wallace was genuine and deep, and he was at the end of his career the man that he had been at the start. This is the heart of her reconciliation, her affirmation of hope. But for Peggy, like her father, none of this came without a price.

In the end, *The Broken Road* is a multilayered memoir, searing in its candor, and if, initially, the life of George Wallace commands our attention, the story of his daughter is nearly as dramatic. We find her there in these same pages as she recounts the sting of a father's neglect, and how she cringed at his ugly treatment of her mother. By her teenage years, things were better in the Governor's mansion, but even then she could feel that something wasn't right. Her father's politics were deeply disturbing, and there were not many people she could talk to about it. "In our family," she said, "no one asked me for my opinion. I really had no voice."

She could share other things with her mother and felt safe in her presence, for Lurleen Wallace was warm-hearted woman, who loved her children and the company of friends, loved to water ski, and fish and find other ways to have a good time. But Lurleen was also dying of cancer. In April 1968, she gave her daughter a pair of diamond earrings to wear to the prom, then died soon afterward on May 7. For a brief time, George Wallace fell apart. He wept in the privacy of his home, and left his daughter to struggle with her grief.

Abruptly, however, he found relief on the campaign trail—a transformation so immediate and sudden that even some supporters found it unseemly. When he ran for president in 1968, Peggy sometimes traveled with him; she loved her father and needed him now as she continued to mourn the loss of Lurleen. But she knew that family was a distant second in his life, compared to the adrenalin rush of politics, and she lived with that truth for the rest of her life. Four years later, she absorbed the shock of the shooting in Maryland, and Wallace's difficulty in coming to terms with it, even as he wrestled with the sins of his past.

Not long after that latest trauma, she made one of the best decisions of her life. She married Mark Kennedy. At first their road together was rocky. Mark as a husband, and later as a father, was everything that

George Wallace was not. He was a listener, for one thing. He actually wanted to know what she thought, and Peggy had trouble believing it was real. She grew detached. Chronic depression stalked her life, worsened by the terrors of migraine headaches, and once when a bad one put her in the hospital, the doctors found a tumor behind her eye.

"That sank in," she remembered, "and my psyche said, 'I've had enough. I think I'll have a little psychotic break.'"

She found herself in a psychiatric ward, screaming at her family for allowing the staff to put her in restraints. It was a long road back, a journey she made with her husband and two sons, and she was grateful for the depth of their understanding. The experience reaffirmed what she already knew: the love of her family was unconditional, and even in times when there was no crisis, they valued the things she had to say. It gave her confidence, reinforcing the belief that she could make it through.

"We were here for her," says Mark, "but Peggy was strong. She pulled herself out of a dark place."

Together, they resumed their journey of conscience, paying homage to Dr. King and embracing the legacy of the civil rights movement. With Peggy's support, Mark became active in politics, running successfully for the Alabama Supreme Court, then serving as chairman of the state Democratic Party. In 2008, they worked and voted for Barack Obama, and on November 5, the day after the election, Peggy wrote an article for CNN in which she offered a startling speculation. If her father were still alive, she wrote, "There is a substantial chance, though not a certainty, that he would put an 'X' by Barack Obama's name."

Because of the recognition that followed, she was invited in the spring of 2009 to participate in an annual celebration of the Bloody Sunday march. In the course of that commemoration, she walked hand in hand with John Lewis, pausing at the summit of the Edmund Pettus Bridge. She remembered the image on the television screen, when she had watched with her mother in the governor's mansion, of a young John Lewis in a tan trench coat, absorbing the blows of Alabama State Troopers. Now here he was as a member of Congress, lost, apparently, in thoughts of his own, as they gazed at the swirling brown river below.

"It was as if," she wrote, "the water was . . . washing away the pain of the past and giving me the courage to step away and find my true self. 'Well, sister,' John finally said, 'Guess it's time for the two of us to move forward. Now you hold my hand 'til we get to the other side.'"

"I found my voice that day," she said. "I made the choice to speak up and speak out every chance I got."

Other extraordinary moments have followed. In 2015, on another anniversary, she found herself on the steps of the Alabama Capitol, holding hands this time with Bernice King. It was easy, again, to get lost in the past, and she reflected on the day in 1963, when Bernice's father, Martin Luther King, had offered his olive branch to the nation. He had proclaimed, improbably, what seemed more like a fantasy than a dream: "One day down in Alabama . . . little black boys and little black girls will be able to join hands with little white boys and little white girls as sisters and brothers."

Almost incredibly, a half century later, she was standing in solidarity with Bernice. "We hugged each other," Peggy remembered, "and I told her I loved her. She said she loved me too. And we do." Later she wrote, "I could not help but wonder how the course of history might have been different if Martin Luther King and Daddy had known that one day, right down here in Alabama, that little black girl and little white girl holding hands would be their own daughters."

All of this has given her a sense of purpose, and as an advocate for peace and social justice, she has raised her voice in multiple settings—at universities and churches and civil rights celebrations, and sometimes before delegations from Congress. Doug Tanner, a Methodist minister and founding director of the Faith and Politics Institute in Washington, has been the architect of some of those appearances. "I've seen her move congressional audiences to tears," he says, "and as a writer, she has opened a window onto tragedy and shame—and in a profoundly personal way, the possibility of redemption."

But redemption, inevitably, is haunted by the past, and she has seen the through line from the worst of Wallace to the presidency of Trump. She knows the dread that many of us feel—a fear that maybe the last fifty years have produced a perfect storm of division from which it will be hard for the country to heal. And on the issues she cares about most, the racial justice her father once opposed, she has seen the threat to hard-earned progress. But she holds on to hope. She believes it is possible for decency to triumph. She has seen it before. This is the lesson she learned with her father, even as she understood what it cost.

The Rabbi and Dr. King

> This account about one of the great friendships of the civil rights era appeared in *Alabama Heritage*, an award-winning quarterly dedicated to the notion that history is best understood as a story.

Martin Luther King Jr. was not at the Bloody Sunday march in Selma. On March 7, 1965—the day that Alabama State Troopers and mounted sheriff's deputies beat demonstrators in a cloud of tear gas—King was preaching at his church in Atlanta. In the hurt and anger that followed, some in the ranks of the civil rights movement bitterly criticized Dr. King for his absence, and even after he rushed to the scene, things at first did not go well.

The following Tuesday he led a march of two thousand people across the Edmund Pettus Bridge, retracing the path of the Bloody Sunday protest. Again, state troopers blocked their advance. By prior agreement, brokered by the U.S. Community Relations Service, King and the marchers knelt to pray, then sang "We Shall Overcome," before King turned around and led the demonstrators back into Selma. More outrage greeted this decision. Leaders of the Student Non-Violent Coordinating Committee labeled the protest "Turnaround Tuesday." They denounced King for his "trickery," for they had not known in advance of his plan to avoid another bloody confrontation. Some vowed never to work with him again.

As the movement threatened to disintegrate, King sent out a call for reinforcements. One of those who answered was Rabbi Abraham Heschel, a Polish refugee, Holocaust survivor, and New York seminary professor. King was grateful to Heschel for his support, just as he was grateful to all the clergy who answered his summons to Selma. Their presence affirmed the moral gravity of the cause, and no one embodied gravity more than Heschel.

King had long admired this Rabbi, ever since reading his book *The Prophets* (Harper & Row, 1962), which was about voices of justice from an ancient time. "The prophet is a man who feels fiercely," Heschel had written. "God has thrust a burden upon his soul, and he is bowed and stunned by man's fierce greed.... God is raging in the prophet's words."

King thought he saw some of that raging in Heschel, tempered, perhaps, by a gentle disposition and twinkling sense of humor. But there was a gravitas—a theological grounding—that King understood and turned to now in a difficult time. On March 21, when, for a third time, civil rights demonstrators set out to march from Selma to Montgomery, protected this time by a federal court order against state interference, King asked Heschel to walk beside him. An iconic photograph resulted: King with Ralph Abernathy on his right and Ralph Bunche and Heschel on his left.

For many years, a journalist in Selma often heard the story—apocryphal, perhaps, for it was difficult to track down—of a little African American boy standing with his mother on the side of the road, as the line of protesters approached.

"Look, Mama," said the little boy, pointing at Heschel, "I think it's God."

Whether or not the story is true, it was told for a time as a kind of civil rights parable about the sacredness of the cause—and the relationship between Heschel and King. This rabbi from Poland, with his flowing white beard and his love of scripture, seemed to embody King's own leap of faith that God himself was present in history—and was present especially in the civil rights movement.

"For many of us," Heschel wrote after Selma, "the march from Selma to Montgomery was about protest and prayer. Legs are not lips and walking is not kneeling. And yet our legs uttered songs. Even without words, our march was worship. I felt my legs were praying."

The friendship between King and Heschel began on January 14, 1963, when both were speaking at the National Conference on Religion and Race held in Chicago, Illinois. In his address Heschel began with what seemed at first to be a touch of humor, but his words quickly turned serious: "At the first conference on religion and race, the main participants were Pharaoh and Moses.... The outcome of that summit meeting has not come to an end. Pharaoh is not ready to capitulate. The exodus began, but is far from having been completed. In fact, it was easier for the children of Israel to cross the Red Sea than for a Negro to cross certain university campuses."

Leaning into his subject, Heschel argued that the mere concept of race was an invitation to the evil of racism, which he regarded as "man's gravest threat to man."

"Religion and race," he asked rhetorically, "how can two be uttered together? To act in the spirit of religion is to unite what lies apart, to remember that humanity as a whole is God's beloved child. To act in the spirit of race is to sunder, to slash, to dismember the flesh of living humanity. Is this the way to honor a father: to torture his child?"

Heschel could not have been surprised that his words resonated with King. There was an urgency about the rabbi's message that King certainly shared. But more than that, their similar understanding of biblical history was apparent from the start. Ever since the Montgomery Bus Boycott, King had used the analogy of Exodus—the Old Testament story of Pharaoh and Moses—and the struggle of the Jewish people to be free. And in the summer of 1963, seven months after the meeting in Chicago, he delivered his "I Have a Dream" speech in Washington, D.C., quoting from the prophet Amos: "No, we . . . will not be satisfied until justice rolls down like waters and righteousness like a mighty stream."

As it happened, this was one of Heschel's favorite verses. He had written about Amos in the first chapter of *The Prophets*, casting him as a man who regarded injustice as a "catastrophe." Amos raved, wrote Heschel, "as if the whole world were a slum," but there was a flipside to the prophet's wrath—God's wrath—at the cruelty and suffering he saw in the world. There was always hope—always God's inexplicable promise of nobler possibilities to come.

Three months after the March on Washington, King and Heschel met again, this time at the United Synagogue of America Golden Jubilee Convention, where King spoke against the oppression of "my brothers and sisters who happen to be Jews in Soviet Russia." As the friendship between the two men deepened, they began to explore an affinity more subtle than the politics of faith: the passionate demand for social justice that initially brought them together. The roots of that concern, they were starting to see, began with a common understanding of God.

The rabbi's daughter, Susannah Heschel, chair of Jewish Studies at Dartmouth College, wrote that her father and King shared "a fundamental assumption of divine concern with the events that are transpiring in the Civil Rights struggle. God is involved and engaged in that struggle, because God is not remote and transcendent, but . . . is affected by the treatment human beings accord one another, . . . suffering with us."

Neither man came to that conclusion easily. The history of Jews, like the history of African Americans, was riddled with pain—a fact they both understood intellectually, as well as personally. They knew it was fair to ask why a benevolent God would permit it. Why would he allow his people to suffer? For Heschel and King, the journey to an answer involved personal moments of anguish.

Heschel narrowly survived the Holocaust. He was born in Warsaw in 1907, the son of a rabbi whose congregation consisted primarily of impoverished Jews. Raised amid the piety of his Hasidic family, he soon sought to broaden his view of the world. As a teenager, he published a volume of Yiddish poetry, then studied in Berlin, regarded at the time as the intellectual capital of Europe. He pursued his doctorate at the University of Berlin, where he wrote a dissertation he later expanded into his book, *The Prophets*.

These were terrible times in Europe, and Heschel would soon see suffering on a scale that he had simply never imagined. He witnessed Hitler's accession of power on January 30, 1933, followed soon after by the Reichstag fire and the infamous book burning at the University of Berlin. He continued to write and lecture in Germany until October 1938, when he and other Polish Jews were expelled. Susannah Heschel wrote:

> Suddenly, in the middle of the night, the Gestapo arrived and gave him one hour to pack two suitcases. He quickly gathered his manuscripts and books and then carried two very heavy suitcases through the streets of Frankfurt to police headquarters, where he was held overnight in a tiny cell. The next morning he was put on a train packed with deported Jews. He told me he had to stand for the duration of a three-day journey to Poland. Denied entry into Poland, the Jews were held at the border in the miserable conditions, many remaining for months. The local Poles refused to give the Jews food. My father was fortunate: his family soon secured his release, and he joined them in Warsaw.

Heschel survived the Holocaust—like "a brand plucked from the fire," he said—when he was offered a teaching position at the Hebrew Union College in Cincinnati, Ohio. But his mother and three of his sisters were killed by the Nazis. Arnold Eisen, chancellor of the Jewish Theological Seminary in New York, where Heschel came to teach after his time in Cincinnati, thought the rabbi must have been "plagued by doubt," rocked in his certainty of "God's presence in the world," after the monstrous crimes of Adolf Hitler. How could it have been otherwise? Heschel, said Eisen, "had lost almost his entire family in the Holocaust."

Eisen was nineteen years old, a student journalist at the University of Pennsylvania, when he and Heschel met. He came to the rabbi's study in New York, having summoned the courage to ask for an interview, and found himself "surrounded by books, floor-to-ceiling books, with barely enough room to stand or sit, with this figure with a long white beard, looking very prophetic, but with kind and twinkling eyes."

The two of them talked about hard things, including the Holocaust, and Heschel told him, "You have doubts [about God]. I do too." But somewhere on the other side of his doubts and his anguish, the rabbi made his great leap of faith. In his book *Israel: An Echo of Eternity* (Farrar, Straus and Giroux, 1969), Heschel wrote, "Our people's faith in God at this moment in history did not falter. At this moment in history Isaac was indeed sacrificed, his blood shed. We all died in Auschwitz, yet our faith survived. We knew that to repudiate God would be to continue the Holocaust."

King, as Heschel would learn, had embarked on a similar journey of faith. As a student of theology at Boston University and Crozer Theological Seminary, King had written skeptically of philosophers from Aristotle to Paul Tillich (whose conceptions of God were, he thought, grand but ultimately "devoid of consciousness and life"). As his biographer Lewis Baldwin has noted, King was a product of the African American church, whose belief in a personal God grew stronger during the early years of the civil rights movement.

King himself remembered a moment in 1956 when the God of history in whom he believed—the God who embraced the cause of justice, even in the midst of human suffering—suddenly and quietly became more real. On January 26, during the early weeks of the Montgomery Bus Boycott, King was arrested and thrust into the back of a police car. He noticed, to his horror, that the cruiser was headed straight out of town. As they crossed the muddy waters of the Alabama River, he could imagine himself floating face down, a police bullet lodged in his brain. Such things happened to Black men in the South. He was trembling badly, and he was embarrassed by his fear, when the police car finally turned around and took him to the jail. This time they only meant to scare him.

King was barely twenty-seven years old, and as he sat alone on the following night, brewing a pot of coffee in his kitchen, he worried that maybe he was out of his depth. The telephone rang. It was a white man threatening his life. King hung up the phone. He could feel a prayer taking shape in his mind, not really a plea for divine intervention, just some words of desperation he could not suppress: "Lord, I must confess that I'm weak now. I'm faltering. I'm losing my courage. And I can't let the people see me like this."

He said he heard an inner voice reply, telling him simply to keep the faith and do what he must, and he would never be alone. The following Monday, January 30, he was speaking at a mass meeting when an old woman rose from one of the pews to say the preacher looked troubled this night. King recognized Mrs. Pollard right away—Mother Pollard, some people called her, a community elder known for her eloquence and a kind of folk wisdom that set her apart. "My feets is tired, but my soul is rested," she had said, declaring her support for the bus boycott. Now she put her arms around King and told him not to worry. "God's gonna take care of you," she said.

For King it was a moment of truth, and nine years later, when he and Heschel arrived in Selma, they shared an assumption of divine concern—a faith in which a personal communion between God and man often took unexpected forms. After the march, Heschel wrote a letter to King affirming his view that the protest was holy—"a day of sanctification," he said, in which men and women were doing the work of God. This understanding became the heart of their friendship—faith in a God who was not an omnipotent puppeteer, pulling the strings of human history, but one who shared in the suffering of the world and needed, even demanded, the help of human beings to heal it.

It was a view with implications beyond civil rights. Even as they celebrated the Selma triumph and the subsequent passage of the Voting Rights Act of 1965, Heschel and King worried about the war in Vietnam. Heschel was the first to take a public stand, and he quietly urged King to do the same. From the earliest months of escalation, the rabbi was tormented by the war. "How can I pray," he asked rhetorically, "when I have on my conscience the awareness that I am co-responsible for the death of innocent people in Vietnam? In a free society, some are guilty, all are responsible."

"My father was sleepless over Vietnam," Susannah Heschel explained. "He would be up late at night—one, two, three in the morning—couldn't sleep he was so upset. It was on his mind all the time."

In October 1965 Heschel joined John C. Bennett, president of Union

Theological Seminary, in organizing a meeting of one hundred clergy in New York to form an organization called Clergy and Laymen Concerned about Vietnam. King was present at the meeting as well, even though the war posed a difficult problem for him. With the passage of the Civil Rights Act of 1964 and the Voting Rights Act the following year, President Lyndon Johnson had emerged as a friend to the civil rights movement, and many of King's most trusted advisers urged him not to break with the president over Vietnam.

For much of 1966, King agonized about the issue. But in January 1967, he opened a copy of *Ramparts Magazine*, a left-leaning monthly, and saw pictures of Vietnamese children gravely wounded by American napalm. He decided he could keep silent no longer. He talked to Heschel about the possibility of a major speech on the war, sponsored by Clergy and Laymen Concerned, which had become well established as a nonviolent antiwar organization. Heschel and other leaders of the group suggested that he speak at Riverside Church. King was delighted by that idea. There was, he thought, no more majestic cathedral in the country than Riverside, which towered over the Hudson River in upper Manhattan. On April 4, 1967, King ascended the pulpit beneath the great stone arches to deliver the most controversial speech of his career. Heschel stood at his side. Heschel, as he introduced King, said, "Our thoughts on Vietnam are sores, destroying our trust, ruining our most cherished commitments with burdens of shame. We are pierced to the core with pain, and it is our duty as citizens to say no to the subversiveness of our government. ... We are here because our own integrity as human beings is decaying in the agony and merciless killing done in our name."

King sounded similar themes:

> As I ponder the madness of Vietnam my mind goes constantly to the people of that peninsula.... They watch as we poison their water, as we kill a million acres of their crops. They must weep as the bulldozers roar through their areas preparing to destroy the precious trees. They wander into the hospitals, with at least twenty casualties from American firepower for one "Viet Cong"-inflicted injury. So far we may have killed a million of them—mostly children.

In the short run, King's speech was greeted with a cascade of scorn. *Life* magazine called it "a demagogic slander that sounded like a script from Radio Hanoi." And the *Washington Post* editorialized: "Many who have listened to him with respect will never again accord him the same confidence. He has diminished his usefulness to his cause, to his country, and to his people."

Heschel's support for King never wavered. "Where in America today" he asked, "do we hear a voice like the voice of the prophets of Israel? Martin Luther King is a sign that God has not forsaken the United States of America. God has sent him to us. His presence is the hope of America."

The year 1968 found King traveling the back roads of Alabama and other parts of the South, trying to build support for a Poor People's March on Washington. In his private moments, he was depressed. The war raged on in Vietnam, and despite the gains of the civil rights movement, he sensed the racial divide in America growing deeper. "I am sorry to have to say," he had concluded, "that the majority of white Americans are racist." He was also focused on the issue of poverty and the staggering level of income inequality in the richest country on earth.

In these days, he found some solace in his time with Heschel. On March 25, he spoke at a birthday celebration for the rabbi, convened by the Rabbinical Assembly of America, and affirmed that Heschel "is, indeed, a truly great prophet." Heschel, in response, invited King and his wife to participate in a family Passover Seder, scheduled for April 16. "The ritual and celebration of that evening seek to make present to us the spirit and the wonder of the exodus from Egypt," Heschel wrote. "It is my feeling that your participation at a Seder celebration would be of very great significance."

King never made it to the Seder. On April 3 in Memphis, Tennessee, speaking in support of a strike by sanitation workers, and reaching deep for the faith to overcome his depression, King evoked the spirit of Exodus, declaring that he had "seen the Promised Land." He compared the civil rights movement to the burning bush from which God spoke to Moses: "Bull Connor next would say, 'Turn the firehoses on . . .' Bull Connor didn't know history. He knew a kind of physics that somehow didn't relate to the transphysics that we knew about . . . the fact there was a certain kind of fire that no water could put out."

The following day King was murdered on his motel balcony, and Rabbi Heschel rushed to Atlanta to speak at the funeral of his friend. In his grief he reaffirmed things he had already said about King's divinely inspired life.

In the years since then, Susannah Heschel, among others, has continued to marvel at the friendship between her father and King, an intimacy that was rooted in faith—a prophet's agony in a sinful world, where the arc of the moral universe is long, and God's justice looms just out of reach.

Bishop Tutu
"The Blasphemy of Apartheid"

In 1986, when the fate of apartheid was still unclear, South African archbishop Desmond Tutu set off on a speaking tour in the United States. To some of us who saw him, our secular understanding of apartheid—our fear and loathing of the South African government (which still, at the time, enjoyed the support of U.S. president Ronald Reagan)—gave way to Tutu's leap of faith; his remarkable certainty that the racial oppression in his country was doomed. I wrote this story for the *Charlotte Observer*.

It was important, I think, that we saw him in a church, the ovation gaining strength as he made his way down the aisle, the choir singing, the applause reverberating off the seven-story ceilings, as he ascended the pulpit and waited for the quiet.

It didn't come right away. There seemed to be a certain hunger in the crowd. Many of them had waited for two and three hours outside the Duke University Chapel, as the evening turned colder and the wind whipped and rattled through the empty oak branches.

Bishop Desmond Tutu was late again. That had been his condition off and on during a tightly scheduled American tour, and on that day—January 19, 1986, the eve of the first Martin Luther King holiday—he had spent the afternoon at Ebenezer Baptist Church in Atlanta, where King had been the pastor.

Even in the pared-down coverage of the network news you could feel a moral yearning that seemed to haunt the day. It was more than nostalgia, though that was part of it—the feeling that the voice of King had never been replaced, not in America anyway.

But the turmoil of South Africa—the black-and-white collision between political reality and the demand for simple justice—had thrust forth a leader in whose unassuming eloquence many Americans could hear the echoes of King.

Tutu, like King, is a Christian minister first of all. His faith is filled with political implications, and his hatred of apartheid, the defining reality of his day-to-day life, is strong and deeply personal. But his response to that reality—the lens through which he sees it, the images and metaphors with which he gives it shape—all come from his religion.

That was never more apparent than at the Duke chapel, as his rhetoric took flight beneath the great Gothic arches.

"You remember," he declared, in accents tracing to the old British Empire,

> that lovely piece in the book of the prophet Jeremiah, who is retiring, sensitive, scared of being a prophet. And God says to Jeremiah, Before I formed you in the womb, I knew you. Hey, Jeremiah. You are not an accident. You are not a divine afterthought. I knew you from all eternity and you are part of my divine plan, and none but you can fulfill the part that I have set aside for you. You are unique.
>
> God was saying to Jeremiah what he says to us in Ephesians—that he chose us in Christ before the foundation of the world. Sometimes we may look like accidents, but none of us is an accident. He blew into us the breath of life, so that forever afterwards each one of us became a God-carrier. Each one of us had to be treated with deep reverence. Each one of us was fragile, God carrying us in the palms of his hands. Each one of us was God's viceroy, God's partner.
>
> And so the evil of the system at home is not so much the pain and the anguish that it causes—great as these must be, as they indeed are. The awful thing about apartheid, the most blasphemous thing about it is when it makes the child of God doubt that they are a child of God. And so the most subversive thing about our faith is that it can say to someone who has their dignity rubbed in the dust and trampled underfoot, "Hey, you know something, Mama," that old lady walking down the dusty streets of Soweto, whose name is not known by her employers because they say her real name is too difficult and so they will call her Annie, Mama, as you walked down the street and they ask, who is that? We can say, "Oh, why that's God's partner."

The media, of course—reporters and editors whose decisions give weight to certain pieces of reality—are too often skeptical about the soaring imagery of the spirit, and so their quotes and questions tend to squeeze the story, to reduce it to politics, as they ask Tutu's opinions about sanctions against his government, or if he believes that revolutionary violence is ever justified.

That was how it was at the thirty-minute press conference that followed his speech at Duke—eighty or more reporters shouting for recognition. Tutu answered their questions, patiently, as he knew he must. His answers were facile, quotable, and usually blunt: "My own position is that all violence is evil. OK? I am opposed to all violence. But the primary violence in South Africa—the terrorism in South Africa—is the terrorism of apartheid." Or: "Those who invest in South Africa buttress one of the most vicious systems the world has known. If you want to know what blacks think, 70 percent of blacks call for sanctions. Let people not use us for an alibi for not doing what they ought to do."

Such quotes, when they are fresh, provide the hook and the hard edge for news stories. They dominate the headlines, and in the public perceptions—the implicit media characterizations that form as a result—Bishop Tutu is transformed into a political leader: Nelson Mandela in clerical collar, wrapping his politics in the rhetoric of the church.

The perception is upside down: Tutu's Christian witness is not a veneer. It is his starting point, and the political implications are merely consequences.

Therefore, he warns, the church must ultimately keep its distance from political organizations—preparing itself to proclaim to any of them. "Thus saith the Lord." But its most important mission is much larger than that: it is to hold aloft for everyone, even those who don't particularly want to see it, a vision of what is possible, the good news of a victory already won.

"The scriptures," Tutu declares,

> say we have a God who forever picks sides. Yesterday, today and forever—a God who chooses to be on the side of the oppressed, of the hungry, the homeless. He scandalizes always. And he says to his church, "You have to be where I will be. You want to know where I am? When I was hungry, you fed me. When I was naked, you clothed me. When I was thirsty, you gave me to drink. When I was sick you visited me. When I was in prison you came to see me.' And when they say, 'Lord, when did we see you and do these things?' he says, 'Yes, inasmuch as you did it to the least of these my brethren and my sisters, you are not doing it just to them. They were me."
>
> And so we are able to say to the perpetrators of injustice and oppression everywhere in the world, "You have already lost. You have lost. How can you take on God?"
>
> And God is saying to all of us—"You are my partners. Will you help

me? So that we can have more compassion, more caring, more justice, more peace, more laughter, more fellowship, more holding to one another, black and white, knowing that we can survive only together, that there cannot be any true freedom for anyone until all are free. You will help me, won't you?" So that the kingdom of this world will become as the kingdom of our God and of his Christ. And he shall reign forever. Amen.

As they cheered him at Duke, as the applause swelled and filled up the room, you couldn't escape the feeling of an awareness deeply stirred: a sense that we are all too much the prisoners of what is, and many political leaders—whether revolutionaries or the perpetrators of oppression—are caught up inextricably in the ugliness of reality. They simply come to mirror the worst in each other. Thus the hunger seems to be for a different kind of vision—for the moral men and women in the middle, the Gandhis, the Kings, and the Desmond Tutus, who proclaim despite the evidence that violence, inhumanity, and all the bewildering complexities and rationalizations of our systems of injustice do not have to triumph.

Epilogue

Desmond Tutu, who died in 2021, was one of four Nobel Peace Prize winners produced by the antiapartheid struggle in South Africa. He joined the freedom fighter Albert Luthuli and was followed by Nelson Mandela, the first president of a new South Africa, and F. W. de Klerk, the country's last apartheid president, who negotiated the end of his own regime.

A Prophetic Journalist

> In the 1980s, I interviewed Jacobo Timerman, one of the great journalists of the twentieth century, and wrote about him in the *Charlotte Observer*, and in my books, *Prophet from Plains: The Legacy of Jimmy Carter* and *The Books That Mattered: A Reader's Memoir*. This essay is adapted from those writings.

In the spring of 1985, Jacobo Timerman was eager to talk about Jimmy Carter, a president without whose intervention Timerman was sure he would have died. He had been a crusading journalist—the editor of *La Opinion*, an opposition newspaper in Buenos Aires, which had set out bravely in the 1970s to expose the excesses of the Argentine government. The country had splintered into violence, with right-wing death squads, and left-wing guerillas, and a military government that, in its struggle against terrorism, became terrorist itself. Between 1976 and the end of the decade, as many as thirty thousand Argentinians simply disappeared—spirited away in the night, or sometimes in broad daylight, in sinister Ford Falcons with no license plates.

Timerman's outcry against that abuse infuriated Ramon Camps, the swaggering police chief in Buenos Aires. In 1977, on an April morning at dawn, twenty men burst into his apartment and led him away in handcuffs. They threw him to the floor of a black sedan, a blanket tossed roughly over his head, and when they stopped, one of the men put a revolver to Timerman's temple. "I'm going to count to ten," he said. "Say goodbye, Jacobo dear." When the counting stopped the man simply laughed, but soon the torture began in earnest—beatings, electrical shocks, solitary confinement for weeks at a time. But the most disconcerting thing, Timerman said—curiously enough, as he looked back on it—was that one of his captors hated him for being a Jew.

In his memoir, *Prisoner without a Name, Cell without a Number*, he offered this account of his torture: "I keep bouncing in the chair and moaning as the electric shocks penetrate my clothes. During one of these tremors, I fall to the ground, dragging the chair. They get angry, like children whose game has been interrupted, and again start insulting me. The hysterical voice rises above the others: 'Jew . . . Jew . . .'"

Timmerman survived his thirty-month imprisonment, which ended in the autumn of 1979, largely he believes, because of the human rights diplomacy of President Carter. Five years after his release, he and Carter met, visiting together at the U.S. Embassy in Buenos Aires. A year after that, Timerman told me about their encounter: "We were looking at each other. We are almost the same height, and our faces were at the same level. I said to him, "How do you feel looking into my face, knowing that you saved my life?" His face flushed red, and he looked down and then he touched my shoulder. We Latins, we are used to embracing. But he is an American, a very shy person, and yet you could see that he was moved. He was practically trembling."

For Timerman it was a moment out of time, an instant, he said, when history seemed to lose its grip and hope and justice became something real. But he had no illusions that it would last. "It was the first time, and I fear the last," he concluded, "in this violent and criminal century that a major power has defended human rights all over the world." This so often had been his experience, those scattered, unexpected moments of light (this one, offered by a leader rejected by the voters of his own country) in a world overpowered by darkness and dread.

In the end, all he knew to do was bear witness.

For most of his life, he had lived in the shadow of violence. He spent his first five years in Bar, a Ukrainian village where the Jewish minority carried an ancient memory of genocide. In 1648, the Cossack chieftain Chmielnitski descended on the town and murdered all the Jews he could find. Writing in 1981, Timerman offered this history of Bar and the way it shaped his view of the world:

> The community . . . assumed that something as brutal as the existence of Cossack murderers could only be God's final test before the coming of the messiah. So staunch was that conviction that in 1717 they constructed their Great Synagogue, receiving permission beforehand from the bishop. I attended that synagogue with my father, his six brothers, and all my cousins, and bear within me still a vague longing for those tall, bearded, unsmiling men.
>
> In 1941, when the Nazis entered Bar, they set that synagogue on fire,

burning many Jews to death. All the other Jews of Bar plus others from the environs, including the Timermans . . . were killed by the Nazis in October of 1942. Some twelve thousand within a couple of days. My father, happily, had left for Argentina in 1928.

Growing up in South America, Timerman became a passionate Zionist, by which he meant not only the creation of a Jewish homeland—a necessity in the wake of Hitler's Holocaust—but also a love of generosity and justice, a worldwide struggle for human freedom. "I became destined for a world I would never abandon," he wrote, "that world, unique in its beauty and martyrdom, that mythology of pain and memory, that cosmic vision imbued with nostalgia."

Such irrepressible idealism pushed him toward a career in writing, and for more than thirty years he plied his trade as a journalist. When he left South America following his release from prison, he set out for the land of his Zionist dream. Coming to Israel, he did find sanctuary for a time. He wrote his memoir of torture and survival, and perhaps as much as anything else he let himself feel the pull of the land. He found so much that was beautiful there, so much history, so much to love. His son had been living on a kibbutz, or farming collective, coaxing crops from what had once been a desert. It was a tradition deeply rooted in Israeli history, when Jews at the turn of the twentieth century began to repatriate Palestine—a journey of escape from the persecutions of Europe.

Timerman recognized the necessity of such a journey. He regarded the modern state of Israel, whatever its flaws, as a beacon of hope to Jews everywhere—and perhaps to other peoples as well, for there was an idealism about its founding, a commitment not only to self-defense, to the prevention of atrocities like those under Hitler, but also to justice. Israelis fought wars when they were attacked, but only then, for they were people who wanted only peace. They understood the horrors of war too well.

But almost as soon as he arrived, Timerman said he could feel a shift—not only in the political climate but in the moral climate as well. In the end, he decided, they were one and the same. In 1982, the Israeli general Ariel Sharon orchestrated an invasion of Lebanon, a massive bombardment that reduced entire city blocks to rubble. There had been raids on Israel from across the border, where Arab radicals had taken refuge. But Timerman was shocked by the scale of Israel's response.

As a passionate Zionist, and as a Jew, for that was how he defined himself, he decided he could not keep silent. Even as his son went off to fight, he wrote an article for the *New Yorker*, which filled almost the entire magazine.

"Many things," he wrote, "were occurring for the first time. For the first time Israel had attacked a neighboring country without being attacked; for the first time it had mounted a screen of provocation to justify a war. For the first time Israel brought destruction to entire cities: Tyre, Sidon, Damur, Beirut."

And also this:

> Every Jew carries within him some old or recent scar from an inflicted humiliation. Heroism is a daily need, and in those first days it came in bundles. But afterward one had to decide whether those burning ruins of Lebanese cities had anything to do with heroism, or whether they were pictures of another war to demonstrate what Jews would be incapable of doing.
>
> A man walks among those ruins, carrying in his arms a child of ten. A group of men, women, and children with their arms raised are under guard, and the expression on their faces, what their eyes say, is easily understood by almost any Jew. Yet we are forbidden to equate today's victims with yesterday's, for if this were permitted, the almost unavoidable conclusion would be that yesterday's crimes are today's.

When I read those words, I found myself thinking of Abraham Heschel, a twentieth-century rabbi, and his book about the Hebrew prophets. "A prophet is a lonely man," Heschel had written. "His standards are too high, his stature too great, and his concern too intense for other men to share." In particular, Heschel concluded, these ancient Hebrew champions of justice expected better things of the Jews, God's chosen people.

Timerman shared the prophets' perspective, and as he spoke of such matters, our formal interview, as sometimes happens, began to morph toward conversation. He asked if I had ever seen the Holy Land, and I told him that yes, in fact, I had. In 1983, when I was working for the *Charlotte Observer*, I had traveled to Israel and the Palestinian territories to speak with ordinary people about peace. I had found a deep yearning for a day when the killing would stop—but also a fear that kept people apart.

Two interviews stood out from the rest. The first occurred on the Palestinian West Bank near the Jewish settlement of Efrat, which was then only partially complete. I was traveling with a Palestinian guide, Ibrihim Mater, a middle-class Arab Christian, regarded by most Palestinians as a moderate. "I can sympathize with the Jewish people and their desire for a home," he said, as his van rumbled down a dusty back road. "Given the history of the Holocaust, I can understand and sympathize. But why at my expense? I did not persecute the Jews, yet I am asked by the world to pay the price for the Holocaust. It is not farfetched to say that the Palestinians are the last victims of Hitler. So we ask, on what piece of land does our right as human beings begin?"

As the van approached Efrat, Israeli steam shovels were hard at work. They had completed a ditch for a new water line, cutting across a field of grapevines that belonged to Palestinians in the village of El Khader. Within the ditch, the frayed ends of grape roots were visible. Farther up the hill, the bulldozers and steam shovels were building a road, and again the first casualties were the fledgling rows of grapes. Some were uprooted, others crushed by the boulders and debris.

But a hundred yards away, in the same rocky field, a sixty-year-old Palestinian named Mohammad Ishmael Elammani was proceeding quietly with the business of his day. He was plowing—moving slowly behind a sway-backed mule, while his wife and two daughters were tilling nearby. Elammani said he was certain the Israelis would take the whole field, but he continued to work it because, "What else do we do?"

"If they take the land by force, let them," he said. "We will not give it up. My father and grandfather and my grandfather's father all worked this same land. Since God created the Earth this land has been in our family. We will never leave it. Taking away the land is taking away your soul."

Having said his piece, Elammani resumed his plowing, while his daughter, Yamneh, put the case more bitterly. "In this place," she said, "we have seen many governments. The Turks, the Jordanians. Only the Israelis have taken away land."

Later that day, in a small café in Jerusalem, I described that scene to one of Israel's military heroes. In 1967, General Mattityahu Peled was coordinator of logistics for Israel's stunning victory in the Six-Day War. He was born in Haifa in 1923, and grew up in Jerusalem. During the early struggle for Israel's liberation, he was a member of the Palmach, among the most elite and dedicated of Jewish freedom fighters. After the creation of the Jewish state, he rose to the rank of general in the Israeli army and served for a time as governor of the occupied Gaza territory. But on what he called "the seventh day of the Six-Day War," he began to find himself at odds with his government. As soon as the war was over, he proposed that Israel adopt as its official policy "the principle of partition"—the basic 1948 proposal of the United Nations to divide the old area of Palestine into two contiguous states, one Jewish and the other Palestinian.

When the Arab states rejected that idea in 1948 and launched a war to eradicate Israel (there would be others), Jordan seized control of the Palestinian West Bank. But Israel took it away in 1967, and Peled saw in that a golden opportunity: to pursue the creation of a Palestinian state that would serve as a buffer with Jordan and a key to peace with the Palestinians.

For about two years, he said, the idea was seriously debated. But in 1969, when Golda Meir became prime minister, the policy shifted irrevocably away from supporting a Palestinian state toward building Jewish settlements on the West Bank. In the years since then, Israel had increased the scale of occupation, building more settlements, and driving up the level of Palestinian rage. In the process, it created for itself an array of dismal options: absorbing, subjugating, or expelling more than a million Palestinians—and then in 1982, launching a preemptive war on Lebanon, where Arab fighters had found sanctuary.

"There is a sentiment," Peled said, "that if you sacrifice a non-Jew to a Jewish interest, it is perfectly moral. But we are killing our own culture. It is impossible to reach a solution based on Israel as the master race.... If it goes on like this, it will signal the end of the Zionist dream."

Jacobo Timerman shared Peled's fear, for they shared the same understanding of the dream—an idea, as Timerman had written, "unique in its beauty and martyrdom, that mythology of pain and memory, that cosmic vision imbued with nostalgia."

Now so much of it seemed to be at risk.

"Yesterday's crimes," Timerman repeated, as our interview drew to a close. He did not mean, of course, to equate the devastation caused by Israel—in Lebanon or on the West Bank—with the massive atrocities committed by Hitler, or the crimes against Jews down through the ages. He condemned Arab terror against the Jewish state. But he worried about the Israeli government, and the heartbreaking images he could not ignore.

There were some in Israel who regarded Timerman as an ingrate. How could he criticize a country that granted him asylum? Others saw him as remarkably brave. Timerman, I think, merely saw himself as a writer—perhaps a feeble calling in the end—trying somehow to issue a warning against the startling human capacity not to learn.

Epilogue, 2023

Jacobo Timerman returned to Argentina in 1984, and two years later, testified at the trial of Ramon Camps, the fallen chief of police in Buenos Aires, who presided over the torture of political prisoners. Timerman wrote two more books on Latin America, one about Cuba under Castro, the other about Chile under the dictator Augusto Pinochet.

Timerman died in 1999.

In Israel, meanwhile, there is still no peace. As this book goes to press, there has been a new eruption of violence, and thousands of Israelis and Palestinians have died. In 2023, the *New Yorker*, which published Timerman's story on the Lebanon invasion, wrote about the "chaos" visited upon the Israelis by the country's right-wing coalition government, including not only the expansion of West Bank settlements but also proposals to weaken the structure of Israel's democracy. Thousands of Israelis took to the streets in protest.

Between Timerman's writings and today's unrest, there have been multiple tragedies, assassinations, and leadership failures—culminating, on October 7, 2023, with a terrorist attack on Israel by Hamas, arguably the most barbaric act of anti-Semitic violence since the Holocaust. Israel's massive retaliation produced a humanitarian catastrophe in Gaza, home to more than two million Palestinians, half of whom were children.

The possibility of such violence—this moral specter of the absence of peace—lay at the heart of Timerman's warning, emphatically echoed by General Peled.

Mikhail Gorbachev
"A Man of Peace"

> In 1990, as Mikhail Gorbachev was working diligently to end the Cold War—an accomplishment that would win him the Nobel Peace Prize—I traveled twice to the Soviet Union and wrote this story for the *Charlotte Observer* about Gorbachev's aspirations, not only for peace, but for reform—perestroika, he called it, and a freedom to speak that he called glasnost—in his own country. Published today against the backdrop of Vladimir Putin's war on Ukraine, this is a heartbreaking reminder of what might have been.

We set out from the center of town, past the Communist Party headquarters with a statue of Lenin rising in the square—cold and resolute, the rage forever frozen in time. Stavropol seems a good beginning point for understanding, this city of three hundred thousand on the northern slopes of the Caucasus Mountains. Mikhail Gorbachev was born only a few miles away, and he began his career in this unlikely place—a farming community six hundred miles from the seat of power.

On the outskirts of the city, we turn down a patchy, blacktopped road where the pavement narrows to a single lane and potholes are an obstacle course for the driver. Around a curve, we see an old woman whitewashing her house. She is stooped and friendly, wearing a yellow kerchief around her head and a blue print dress, faded, with dark blue socks rolled down around her ankles.

"Ah yes," she says, when we are introduced and begin to ask questions. "I like Mr. Gorbachev very much . . . Why?" She pauses and considers the question. Her expression turns grave as she delivers her answer. "I am a widow. My husband was killed in World War II. Mr. Gorbachev is a man of peace—peace and hope. Those are very important things. But ours is a country with many problems. People have money, but nothing to buy."

She smiles and continues her thought, speaking in a voice that's wistful and sure. "So many, many problems, and some are getting worse. But I wouldn't go back to the way things were."

After two trips to the Soviet Union, and lengthy conversations with dozens of people—drivers and journalists, priests and teachers and Communist Party members, diplomats, farmers, and budding young Soviet entrepreneurs—I decided that brief encounter in Stavropol reflects the mood of the country about as well as any. On the one hand, there is ample room for pessimism and gloom—indeed, those emotions tend to dominate the headlines. The economy isn't working, and ethnic fighting in the Soviet provinces—particularly in Armenia and Azerbaijan—has left hundreds dead and created several hundred thousand refugees. And yet for all of that, there was exhilaration in the air—a sense that something profound is happening, and no one is quite sure where it will end.

"We are seeing things," says our guide in Stavropol, Valentine Mezine, "that most of us never expected to see in our lives."

As Mezine was speaking, we were driving toward the village of Tartarka, where most people work on collective farms, but where also, under Gorbachev's reforms, private farm plots are much more numerous. It was a cold December day. Snow was everywhere, the hillsides shimmering in the bright sunlight. As the car slipped along on the ice-covered roads, Valentine and his driver, Ivan Sergeyevich, suddenly turned up the radio. There was a live report from the Congress of Deputies—the elected parliament then meeting in Moscow. On this particular morning, December 12, the delegates were debating Article 6, the provision of the Soviet Constitution that gives total power to the Communist party. Many of the delegates were seeking its repeal.

"It should be repealed," said Mezine, "but even to have it discussed..."

His voice trailed off into private thoughts, but after a moment, he began to talk of changes—the apparent end of the Cold War, the beginnings of democracy in Eastern Europe, the freedom in his own country to speak and to think. All of those things are a source of pride, and they have, he says, bought Gorbachev time. Mezine is not a typical Russian. He is a highly educated man in his forties, a linguist by trade, gentle, reflective, a voracious reader. Those things tend to set him apart. But he is far from alone in his basic optimism. I asked our driver, Ivan—younger and less educated than Mezine—how he thought perestroika was going.

"Well," he said, "it's going—and where it goes, there we will go too."

Then he glanced back over his shoulder, and in case his answer sounded merely fatalistic, he raised his right fist quickly and smiled.

"There are problems," he said. "But this is still a time of great hope."

It was rush hour in Moscow, a late afternoon snarl of taxi cabs and a few private cars, swerving in and out of the unmarked lanes. As we stopped for a light, just a few blocks from the great walls of the Kremlin, a young man in tattered clothes—obviously drunk, with a single crutch thrust beneath his right arm—waded into the traffic. His eyes were wild and his face unshaven, and he began shouting curses at the people in the cars. Our driver was startled, and harshly blew his horn. The young man whirled and slammed his crutch into the headlight of the car. *Potselui zhopu*, he shouted. Kiss my ass.

As we drove away, our driver seemed embarrassed. "Just another drunk," he muttered. "Very big problem in the Soviet Union."

From the 1960s until Gorbachev came to power in 1985, the consumption of alcohol had quadrupled in the Soviet Union. For Gorbachev, it was a disturbing symptom, a warning sign of a much deeper problem. As he wrote in his 1987 book *Perestroika*, virtually every facet of Soviet life was in need of renewal. The economy was probably most obvious—with indifferent managers, indolent workers, and out-of-date factories producing shoddy goods. But in Gorbachev's view, the economy merely reflected the spirit of the people.

"The initial task," he wrote, "is to wake up those who have fallen asleep . . . to ensure that everyone feels as if he is the master of the country . . . We must unfold the entire potential of democracy."

Gorbachev's critics say he hasn't yet done that. But no one denies there has been a stunning change—an almost startling new freedom to speak that has altered the psychological climate of the country. At least for now.

"Glasnost is real," said an American diplomat. And almost literally, the evidence is everywhere. In Rostov, we met a young man named Ivan Verizov, quiet and thoughtful, who has begun his own business under Gorbachev's reforms. "Lenin's great mistake," he said, "was his embrace of Karl Marx." We asked if he feared retribution for that kind of heresy.

"No," he said. "I believe in glasnost."

Even our guides were blunt and outspoken. One supported religious services in the Kremlin. Another sought the repeal of Article 6, which guarantees a Communist monopoly of power, while a third championed the rights of non-Russian minorities. But it was also true that old habits die hard.

In Stavropol, in a park immediately outside the Communist Party headquarters, we talked with a group of medical students about everything from politics to the once-forbidden topic of religion. A few days later, several students came to the translator, Valentine Mezine, and asked, "Are you sure those people were Americans? Are you sure they weren't from the KGB?"

"That is how we have lived," said Mezine. "But more and more every day, the people believe. It is a change—you can feel it all around.... We have begun to look hard at who we really are."

To get a sense of what that means, it helps to visit Red Square on a cold winter night, when the snow is falling gently in the lights, swirling in the wind, drifting past the tomb of the unknown soldier. The brick streets are empty, except for a few soldiers hunched against the cold and one or two young couples at the gate to Lenin's tomb. Everywhere, there are monuments to the past—Saint Basil's Cathedral, with its multicolored domes and golden crosses, and the ancient brick walls of the Kremlin itself. They are reminders of a history that is rich and flawed—a heritage of suffering, endurance, and faith, and a heritage also that has been split apart. From Stalin through Brezhnev, history was tainted by official ideology, with a repudiation of the church and mythical elevation of the Communist Party.

Now that is changing, and one of the young Russians directly affected is Alexei Ivanovich, a history teacher in a Stavropol school. He is a member of the party—a dark-haired man with a friendly smile, who seems a bit nervous in the presence of Americans. As he begins to talk, beads of sweat pop out of his lip. But he says he is pleased by our interest in glasnost, for it has dramatically altered his life as a teacher—has given him new freedom to search for the truth. He describes in general terms something he has recently been teaching about—an era known as collectivization, when Stalin abolished private ownership of land. Millions died in the famine that followed. In Stavropol alone, the death toll was fifty thousand.

"My grandfather and grandmother suffered," said Alexei, his voice now soft. "It is good to teach about these things."

A few blocks away up the snow-covered sidewalk, we met another staunch believer in glasnost—a man about the same age as Alexei, though his background is different. Bishop Michael is a Russian Orthodox cleric who presides over a church with a new seminary—testament, he says, to a religious renaissance that has taken firm hold in the Gorbachev years. According to official Russian Orthodox figures, at least seventeen hundred new churches have opened in the last two years—a response to Gorbachev's gestures of tolerance, which included, most recently, his meeting with the Pope.

We asked Bishop Michael what he thought of the meeting, and when he paused for a moment to gather his thoughts, I mentioned several interpretations I had read. The first and most common was that the papal meeting was essentially strategic—an attempt by Gorbachev to win the support of Soviet believers, who make up about half of the country's population. But another view that has been advanced now by syndicated columnist Joseph Sobran and by author Mark Helprin in the *Wall Street Journal* is that Gorbachev is a closet believer—baptized at the age of three, raised by a mother who was, and is, a devout churchgoer. Bishop Michael smiled.

"I think," he said, "the truth is probably somewhere in between. I think he appreciates the history of the church—its role in the culture. For a thousand years, it has been part of our life. As the ancient philosopher said, 'the soul of a man is a Christian soul.'"

As the bishop talked, I was struck by the similarity of his views to those of a Communist Party official in Rostov. Gorbachev, the official said, has a quality called *duhovnost*—the Russian word for spirituality. In his efforts to revitalize the country, he has sought to tap into the historic strengths of the people. One of those is the faith and endurance embodied by the church. The other is the spirit of revolution embodied by the party—the belief that the world can really be changed.

"Gorbachev," the official said, "really does have a transcendent vision."

In recent months, however, there have been doubters. The week before he died in December, Andrei Sakharov, the Nobel laureate and human rights activist, worried that Gorbachev's vision had given way to vacillation.

"I see that he is behaving with great indecision," said Sakharov. "Distrust is ripening. I think this distrust is justified."

On a cold day in Moscow, not far from Red Square, an old woman was huddled in an underground walkway. She was dressed in ragged clothes—a faded black coat and checkered shawl pulled tight around her neck. She was bent at the waist, and in her right hand she held out a cup.

Pazhaloosta, she cried, never looking in the eyes of the people who passed. *Pazhaloosta, pazhaloosta*—please help me. Such abject poverty still is not common, but the country's economy is in deep trouble. We visited a Stavropol grocery, where the meat counter was bare except for chicken—including chicken feet, which some Russians use to make soup. Another store in Rostov offered only sausage, with a single piece of beef so full of fat that no one had bought it.

"Outside Moscow," said a diplomat in the U.S. embassy, "people drive two hours to the city to find food."

In a poll in 1989, commissioned by Gorbachev's top economic adviser, more than 90 percent of those surveyed described the economy as either critical or bad; 57 percent said they had no confidence in their economic future. But bad as it is, some say the economy is merely an aggravation—a complicating factor in a much more serious problem that threatens the very future of the Soviet Union. The country has about 290 million people. Of those, only about 145 million are Russian. The rest are divided among more than one hundred nationalities, or distinct ethnic groups—many with grievances against Moscow, and some with blood hatred toward one another.

With glasnost, the unrest has risen quickly to the surface. Some of the country's fifteen republics, especially the Baltic states of Estonia, Latvia, and Lithuania, are headed resolutely in the direction of secession. Most of the rest seek greater independence, and at least one, the Muslim republic of Azerbaijan, is virtually at war with its neighbor, Armenia. The issues seem arcane to the outside world. In the case of Armenia and Azerbaijan, the point of dispute is Nagorno-Karabakh, an Armenian enclave in Azerbaijan that wants to secede and become a part of Armenia. The Azerbaijani resistance to that idea has been led by a group called the Popular Front, based in the ancient city of Baku. For months last year, the front coordinated a series of strikes and blockades, disrupting railroad service to Armenia—including relief supplies for victims of the 1988 Armenian earthquake. Azerbaijani militants blew up bridges to keep the trains from getting through, and there was bitter fighting in the villages near the border. Many Russian liberals, including Andrei Sakharov, have viewed the Popular Front as "extremist." But our Intourist guide in Baku, a young Azerbaijani, praised the group for its essential moderation.

"It is led by very educated people," he said, "doctors, lawyers, people like that. Its support is very broad."

The guide, however, became uneasy when we asked to visit the group's headquarters. "Perhaps you can go yourself," he said. "Perhaps you can find somebody to talk to."

We decided to try it, heading west from the banks of the Caspian Sea, down a narrow street overhung with trees.

"You will know it," said our guide, "by the size of the crowd."

After four of five blocks, we came to an old stone building set back from the road, with the door hanging open and the screens ripped and missing from the windows upstairs. Thirty or forty people were milling outside, and almost immediately they closed in around us. A slender man in his thirties—olive-skinned like the others, with a day's growth of beard—led us inside, where plaster hung from the walls and placards and old banners were piled in a corner.

In a large and barren room upstairs, a handsome man in a pinstriped suit, clearly in charge, demanded to see our identification. He spoke no English, and eventually gave up trying to talk to us. Later, however, a supporter who said his name was Mekhman described the Popular Front position this way: "We have tried to negotiate, but the other side has only one demand. They want our land. Armenians came to Karabakh in the 1820s. It is a large area. It has no border with Armenia. Historically, it is Azerbaijan. We have told them, 'You are welcome to live here, but we are not going to give it away.'"

Then he added in an ominous aside, "We have armed our villages for self-defense."

Soon after our visit, self-defense took the form of naked terror, with Azerbaijanis slaughtering Armenians who live in Baku. The battles soon spread across the republic. All over the Soviet Union, the strife has grown more explosive in the Gorbachev years, and increasingly, it seems, Gorbachev's response has satisfied no one. Many say he has moved too fast, embracing the concept of self-determination and stirring what one American diplomat calls "the ancient Russian fear of chaos." Others say he moves too slow.

In the current issue of *Foreign Affairs*, Polish-born Zbigniew Brzezinski, President Carter's national security adviser, predicts a period of "protracted ethnic violence ... the globe's most acute national conflicts," unless Gorbachev radicalizes his reforms. The only real hope, says Brzezinski, is "the eventual transformation of the Soviet Union ... into a genuinely voluntary confederation."

Before leaving for Moscow in December, I asked Brzezinski if he could imagine the opposite—the Soviet Union simply coming apart. The situation is grave, he said. In some ways, "the dissolution has already begun."

On the outskirts of Leningrad, just a few miles from the Baltic Sea, there is a cemetery called Piskaryovskoye, with carefully tended graves and broad walkways that are covered with stone. A statue of Mother Russia stands guard at one end, and in the background there is music—the Leningrad Symphony of Dimitri Shostakovich. The symphony was written during Hitler's siege, when five hundred thousand people died in three years. For the most part, they are buried together in this one cemetery—in 42 mass graves marked only by the year. The scale of the suffering is hard to comprehend—a half million dead in nine hundred days, all from one city—ten times the number of Americans killed in Vietnam.

As we walked among the graves, and the occasional families placing flowers on the stones, I thought of the old woman in Stavropol, and her instinctive first assessment of Gorbachev's accomplishments: "Mr. Gorbachev is a man of peace."

In a world of diminished Cold War tensions, her answer rang true—a quiet testimonial to the vision of one man. But how far, really, does the vision extend? Can Gorbachev bring peace within the Soviet Union? What about the economy and the future of democracy? Will he support in his own country the kind of multiparty pluralism he has allowed in Eastern Europe?

We put those questions to an official at the U.S. Embassy, who answered on the condition that she not be named. Her prognosis was gloomy. She talked about the economy and opposition in the party, the growing trend toward ethnic violence. Rationally, she said, those are the things you have to talk about—all of that and the ancient Russian yearning for order, its tolerance for authoritarian leaders, many of them ruthless, a few of them crazy, imbedded in history and its DNA. She offered, finally, in tones of admiration, a two-sentence summary of the Gorbachev years: "This man," she said, "keeps on surprising us. But he has chosen a difficult path."

Epilogue

Ten months after this article was published, Gorbachev won the Nobel Peace Prize, primarily for his efforts to end the Cold War. Speaking at the United Nations, he proclaimed the dawn of an era when "the use of force is no longer an instrument in foreign policy"—a declaration both impossibly idealistic and utterly rational, as the world has proven many times since then. Writing about that speech in *Rolling Stone*, journalist Lawrence Wright, among other commentators, reflected in amazement on its implications: "Here was Gorbachev declaring peace."

It was a time of extraordinary hope.

But despite the optimism he inspired in the world, as the Soviet Union continued to unravel, Gorbachev, this "man of peace," was forced to resign. In December 1991, Boris Yeltsin became the new leader of Russia, succeeded in turn by Vladimir Putin, under whom the possibilities that Gorbachev embodied have been replaced by their cold-blooded opposite.

Gorbachev died on August 30, 2022, relatively forgotten in his own land, dismissed by others as one of history's losers. He was ninety-one.

Shaking Hands with Jane Goodall

This reminiscence about a chance meeting with Jane Goodall, and the inevitable reflections that followed, was written specifically for this collection. Prior to this personal encounter, I had followed her story more or less in passing.

Jane Goodall was sixty-eight years old when she came to Charlotte, North Carolina. The ponytail was no longer blond, as it had been that day in the 1960s when she reached out her hand and—ever so gently in the African forest—touched the fingertips of a chimpanzee. But her presence seemed to be unchanged.

My wife Nancy and I had both read her book, *In the Shadow of Man*, recounting her work in Tanzania, where she came to know the wild chimpanzees, and through her studies—and her relationships with our closest living relatives—came to believe in a web of connection, both sacred and fragile, of life on our planet. We were eager to hear her speak, but we also knew from recent experience that even our heroes can be disappointing.

A few years earlier, another icon had come to our city. Mother Teresa was quite literally a modern-day saint, and Nancy and I had been dismayed. We had primed ourselves for a beatific encounter, but in her lecture to an overflow crowd we discovered a bitterness—a didactic, hard, judgmental presence—that took us by surprise. She spoke in passing about the calling that had made her famous—how she came to Calcutta in the 1940s and began her work among the sick and the dying, the people who had no place to live. "The poorest of the poor," she said.

But mostly what she talked about was abortion, which she condemned as "murder by the mother herself." There was, we thought, barely a trace of empathy or compassion for the tragedy inherent at the heart of the issue. Rarely does a woman, when it is personal, approach this subject without feeling the gravity of what she is doing. She may have been raped; her life, medically, may be at risk. But regardless of the specifics, it is almost always, as one theologian would later put it, "a matter of two vulnerable lives." For yes, a helpless life is growing in the womb; a heart soon beats, and not long after, there is a brain that is capable of registering pain. But there is also, almost inevitably, the terrible, private anguish of the mother.

Few issues are more riddled with nuance, and Mother Teresa acknowledged none of this. Instead she managed to present herself as embittered—a woman who, as we would soon learn, was wrestling in the final years of her life with a loss of the faith that had once sustained her: "If there be God—please forgive me. When I try to raise my thoughts to Heaven, there is such convicting emptiness that those very thoughts return like sharp knives and hurt my very soul."

This was the tragedy we could feel in her presence—a life of sacrifice for a God in whom she no longer believed. On her visit to Charlotte, she seemed more than anything else to radiate the darkness—the aridity—that haunted her soul.

Jane Goodall, who had been called by some "the Mother Teresa of environmentalism," proved to be different. We had wondered if this would be so. Goodall, too, had struggled with profound disillusionment—a kind of "eco-grief" about what human beings "with our very big brains" seemed intent on doing to our planet. "We have not just compromised the future of young people," she said. "We've been stealing it."

In a conversation with Mike Collins, a gifted interviewer for Charlotte public radio, Goodall spoke of hard realities, tempered by her reasons for hope. Because of her research and the work of many others, she said, "We now know there isn't a sharp line dividing us from the rest of the animal kingdom. It's a blurry line. And it gives us a little humility. Once you are prepared to believe that we are not the only beings with personalities, minds, and, above all, feelings, it does give you a new understanding of our relationship to the natural world. That's why it's so desperately important to use that understanding to save what's left because we are destroying the world very fast."

In her efforts to spread that message, she has not only lobbied heads of state and other government officials, corporate polluters, and companies using animals in their research but also meets as often as she can with children. This, she says, is the place to plant the seeds of understanding—an epiphany that came in 1991, as she hosted a group of twelve students in Tanzania. They met at her home in Dar es Salaam to talk about their fears for the planet.

At first, they said they felt overwhelmed. The problems were simply too large. But the more they talked, the more they decided that each of them could try to do something, and if enough people around the world did the same, maybe their efforts would multiply. Maybe their example might trickle up. Out of that conversation, in which Goodall listened as much as she spoke, came the idea for Roots and Shoots, an educational program for young people ranging in age from preschool to college. With the help of teachers and other mentors, the students could take on specific problems—environmental, humanitarian—but something more manageable than saving the world. And perhaps in the end the world could be saved.

This was their great leap of faith. Within a few years, there were Roots and Shoots chapters in more than 140 countries. Of the original twelve students who met with Goodall, all became involved in the organization, one grew up to be a national director, another the minister of the environment in Tanzania.

In Charlotte, where more than thirty-five hundred people turned out to hear her, Goodall told that story, and repeated her mantra of possibility—a metaphor of hope that became a common refrain in her speeches: "Roots creep underground everywhere and make a firm foundation. Shoots seem very weak but to reach out to the light they can break open brick walls."

Purely by happenstance, as she was leaving the auditorium, Nancy and I found ourselves only a few feet away from where she was walking. We didn't want to be presumptuous, but one of us—I think it was Nancy—said something like, "Thank you for coming to our city. Your message was important for us to hear. It was our honor."

To our surprise, Jane Goodall stopped. "Thank you for saying that," she replied. "That is just so very kind."

That was it. No extended conversation, just a brief handshake and a few simple words—an exercise in politeness perhaps, and yet somehow it seemed to be more. Even offstage there was something remarkable about Goodall's presence—not only a measured deflection of flattery, something she clearly did not need, but a refusal somehow to set herself apart, an accessibility undiminished by her fame.

As she walked away, Nancy and I were struck by an unexpected clarity. In Goodall's openness and self-possession, we thought we could see why a curious chimp might touch her hand—and why that touch might change the world's understanding of science, and offer a liberating affront to man's understanding of our place on the planet.

In 1960, which proved to be a life-defining year, Goodall went to the Gombe Stream Preserve to study the wild chimpanzees. Already it had been an improbable journey, beginning, in a sense, when she was barely one year old. That was when her mother gave her a stuffed toy—a chimpanzee doll she would call Jubilee, named for a baby chimp born that year in the London Zoo. Already Jane was an animal lover (one of her earliest memories was hiding in a chicken coop to learn how hens went about laying eggs), and as she grew older and began to read, the Tarzan books were some of her favorites. By the time she was eight, as she wrote in her book, *In the Shadow of Man*, "I decided I would go to Africa and live with wild animals when I grew up."

If childhood fantasies most often fade, Goodall's did not. Steadily, in fact, it began to take on the proportions of "a longing," fulfilled, she said, when she was twenty-three and made her first trip to the African continent. In Nairobi, someone told her she should meet Louis Leakey, the world-renowned paleontologist who had spent much of his career studying our earliest human ancestors. Leakey immediately offered her a job, which astonished Jane as she looked back on it. Perhaps it was simply that Leakey, like almost everybody else—from the audiences she would meet worldwide to the chimpanzees of the Tanzanian forests—was captivated by Goodall's air of self-possession, disarming because it was so unassuming. Whatever the case, Leakey not only hired her as a secretary but asked her to go with him and his wife Mary to study the fossils at the Olduvai Gorge.

The Leakeys, in the 1950s, were searching for skeletal fragments from species known as *Australopithecus* and *Homo habilus*, some of the earliest toolmakers on the evolutionary chain. This rocky gorge cutting through the dry Serengeti plains was abundant in its archeological remains, which made it, for Jane, an exciting time to be there. One night in camp, after a dusty day in the field, Leakey began to talk to her about a group of chimpanzees living in a mountainous forest near Lake Tanganyika. There had been few serious studies, none successful, of chimpanzees in the wild. Leakey asked Goodall if she would like to study this group.

Academically, she was unqualified. She had no college degree. But Leakey thought this might be an advantage, for she could approach her subject with an uncluttered mind. When Goodall agreed, Leakey set out to raise money for the project, eventually securing a small foundation grant that would cover the first six months of research. But there was a problem. Leakey also confessed that he was falling in love with her.

As *National Geographic* later reported, Jane was "horrified" by this overture from a married man thirty years her senior—and by the love letters that continued to come even after she had told him no. She also confessed to one of Leakey's biographers that her greatest fear, buried in all the personal awkwardness, "was what my rejection of him might mean for my study of chimpanzees." Leakey, however, never wavered. If his romantic feelings went unrequited, he never ceased to be Goodall's champion—or her confidante as she embarked on her work in the field.

It did not go well at first. For nearly six months, the animals were wary of her presence, disappearing into the forest whenever they sensed her coming too close. She had found a place she called "the Peak," a grassy ridgetop where she would often sit for hours, searching through binoculars for chimpanzees eating figs and other fruit. But whenever she tried to narrow the distance, the animals fled.

She battled through her disappointment and depression, her fear that the mission might end in failure, until finally there came a breakthrough—a series of breakthroughs, actually, all of them, remarkably, involving the same chimpanzee. She had named him David Graybeard because of the color of the hair on his chin. Giving names to the subjects of her research seemed appropriate, for even from a distance she was beginning to see that chimpanzees had distinct personalities. David, she had already noticed, was less afraid of her than the others. He was frequently found in the company of Goliath, a chimpanzee with a "splendid physique," who moved, she thought, with athletic grace.

Late one day, as soft evening shadows descended on the forest, she came upon the two of them together, grooming each other barely twenty yards away from where she was standing. She thought they would run, but they did not. They continued their grooming for fully ten minutes before David stood up and stared at her. She wrote about the moment this way:

> It so happened that my elongated evening shadow fell across him. The moment is etched deep into my memory: the excitement of that first close contact with a wild chimpanzee and the freakish chance that cast my shadow over David even as he seemed to gaze into my eyes. Later it

acquired an almost allegorical significance, for of all living creatures today only man, with his superior brain, his superior intellect, overshadows the chimpanzee. Only man casts his shadow of doom over the freedom of the chimpanzee in the forests with his guns and his spreading settlements and cultivation. At that moment, however, I did not think of this. I only marveled in David and Goliath themselves.

A short time later, she would see David Graybeard again, this time with a small group of chimps eating the carcass of a baby bush pig. Until that moment, it was widely assumed that chimpanzees ate only plants, with, at most, an occasional supplement of insects. Now, it was clear they were hunters, and, as Goodall's observations would establish, their prey included not only bush pigs but several different types of monkeys.

Then came the biggest discovery of all, and once again David Graybeard was her teacher. On one of her wanderings through the forest, Jane found him bending over a termite mound, inserting a stick into a hole and eating the clinging termites as he withdrew it. Later, she saw him break off a twig and strip away the leaves, preparing yet another crude tool to harvest his termite lunch.

Before this, scientists had assumed that only humans were toolmakers—that it was, in fact, one of the lines of demarcation between our species and all others. Increasingly, Goodall was coming to believe that the demarcations were not clear but blurred, and now David Graybeard offered a dramatic moment of proof. For Goodall, as well as her mentor Louis Leakey, the implications were philosophical as well as scientific—a new revelation of the place of human beings in the panoply of life.

Jane sent an excited message, and Leakey responded with a cable: "NOW WE MUST REDEFINE TOOL STOP REDEFINE MAN STOP OR ACCEPT CHIMPANZEES AS HUMAN."

Things happened quickly after that. Based on Goodall's remarkable discovery, Leakey secured funding for her work from the National Geographic Society. In the spring of 1962, also with his support, she gave a presentation at the prestigious Zoological Society of London. Many of those in attendance were mesmerized, but there were doubters. One of the society's officers dismissed her work as "anecdote and speculation" that made "no real contribution to science." An Associated Press reporter began his story about her this way: "A willowy blonde with more time for monkeys than men told today how she spent 15 months in the jungle to study the habits of the apes."

In 1962, such condescension was not uncommon. In that same year in the United States, another woman scientist, Rachel Carson, published a book called *Silent Spring*. She offered it as an urgent warning about the chemical industry and the nation's overuse of pesticides—a danger to the environment, she argued, and a risk to the health of the human population. The chemical industry pushed back, challenging not only her message but her presumption in writing the book in the first place. One industry lobbyist speculated darkly that Carson was "probably a communist" because she was an attractive woman who remained unmarried. "In postwar America," wrote her biographer Linda Lear, "science was god and science was male."

Through it all Carson stood her ground, and the more she was attacked, the more her fame and accolades grew. *Silent Spring* was serialized in the *New Yorker*, endorsed by President John F. Kennedy, and a U.S. Supreme Court justice called it "the most revolutionary book since *Uncle Tom's Cabin*."

Across the Atlantic, Jane Goodall had a similar experience. When British scientists accused her of anthropomorphizing her subjects, giving them names, and projecting—sentimentally, unscientifically—human qualities onto their behavior, Goodall confidently replied that it was they, not she, who had it all wrong. Their insistence on objectifying chimpanzees was, itself, a barrier to understanding—a blinder to the nature of these amazing creatures—these sentient beings who had more in common with man, for good or ill, than our arrogance would allow us to admit. And if this were true of chimpanzees, what about other species in the great web of life?

For Goodall, this developing awareness was soon amplified by a level of fame that took her by surprise. In 1963 she wrote her first cover story for *National Geographic*, "My Life among Wild Chimpanzees," with photographs by Hugo van Lawick, whom she would soon marry. Two years later, after showers of acclaim, a documentary film, "Miss Goodall and the Wild Chimpanzees" aired before an audience of twenty-five million North American viewers. The editors at *National Geographic* saw immediately they were onto something special. This was a feel-good story for the ages, and over the next several decades a flood of articles, books, and documentaries would follow.

The world fell in love with Jane Goodall.

The reality in the African forest, however, was sometimes dark. On one occasion, an outbreak of polio, probably contracted from a nearby village, swept through the population of chimps. For Jane it was a heartbreaking scene as animals she had come to know were crippled or paralyzed by disease. But the most disturbing moment came in 1974. This was the year a territorial war broke out between two groups of chimpanzees, one in an area called Kasekela in the northern part of the Gombe Preserve, and another in Kahama, further to the south. Once again, the horrifying things Goodall witnessed had never been recorded by science. War was, or so the world assumed, the dubious monopoly of man.

The actual reality was gruesome—particularly to Jane, who had come to regard chimpanzees as "rather nicer" than people. *Discover* magazine offered this account, complete with the names she had given the chimps:

> First blood was drawn on January 7, 1974, by a war party of six Kasekela males, who ambushed Godi, a southern male, as he was eating fruit from a tree. The northerners approached silently; Godi was not aware of their presence until it was too late. He jumped down and ran, with the Kasekela males on his heels. A chimp grabbed Godi's legs and threw him to the ground. The other five caught up, then bit, pounded, and stamped on Godi while he was pinned to the ground. After 10 minutes of the whirling tornado of screeching chimps, the northerners left, leaving Godi on the forest floor to die from his injuries.
>
> Over the next four years, more of the Kahama males were picked off in a similar manner. The second victim was beaten to death for 20 minutes by three males. Next was old Goliath, a high ranking male back when the two chimp groups were united. Five Kasekela males, his former friends, turned on him. After the attack, his murderers repeatedly drummed on tree trunks, hurled rocks, and threw branches while calling out, as if in triumph. Goliath died from his wounds the next day.

"For several years," Goodall wrote later, "I struggled to come to terms with this new knowledge. Often when I woke in the night, horrific pictures sprang unbidden to my mind—Satan [one of the apes], cupping his hand below Sniff's chin to drink the blood that welled from a great wound on his face; . . . Figan, charging and hitting, again and again, the stricken, quivering body of Goliath, one of his childhood heroes."

It was a terrible thing to contemplate.

In the end, however, there was also this: if the similarities between humans and our closest relatives involved the sharing of our darkest impulses, still the depth and complexity of Goodall's discoveries had implications for humankind—for our place on a planet so often debased by the arrogance of our understandings.

There soon came a time when Goodall found herself spending less and less time in the African Forest. By the 1980s, she was traveling three hundred days a year, sometimes more, shifting the nature of her vocation from scientist to environmental activist. Having earned a Ph.D. at Cambridge to supplement knowledge acquired in the field, she was, indisputably, *the* foremost authority on chimpanzees. She was determined to assure their survival, which sometimes proved to be to be a heartbreaking mission.

There was, already, a thread of sadness running through her life. Some of it was personal. In 1974, the year of the Great Chimpanzee War, she and her husband Hugo divorced. As a skilled and prolific wildlife photographer, he was powerfully drawn to the Serengeti, those vast Tanzanian plains teaming with elephants, buffalo, and giraffes—as well as lions and other photogenic predators. Jane was committed to her work at Gombe, and in time they simply drifted apart. Their young son Grub stayed with Jane until it was time for him to go to school. At that point, she sent him to England to live with her mother. It was a painful decision, for there was sadness that went with life's priorities—a bittersweet knowledge that she would see her little boy only on holidays, and when he came to Tanzania for the summers.

A decade later, in the 1980s, as Goodall embraced, reluctantly, the moral necessity of her life as an activist, her grief would come in a different form. She missed her time alone in the forests, or spent with her friends, the chimpanzees. These were the happiest years of her life. Nostalgia became a wistful companion. But now, she said, there was something much harder. On her travels to every part of the world, she frequently found herself face-to-face with the cruelties inflicted by humankind. On a visit to a medical research facility, where chimpanzees were used as subjects, she stood in front of a metal cage where a chimp had lived for sixteen years. As she spoke to this unhappy creature, and looked into his eyes, she thought about the lives of chimpanzees she had known in the forest. She could not help herself. Tears welled up and trickled down her cheek. The chimpanzee, whose name was Jo Jo, reached through the bars, and gently, with his forefinger, wiped away the tears.

This somehow brought it all into focus—all the suffering and environmental damage—but also the tender truth of her work. Despite the "eco-grief" she experienced, she knew there was another side to the story. So many people were doing the kind of research she had done—with gorillas, elephants, and dolphins—even mollusks and birds. In 2021, when Jane was eighty-seven, *My Octopus Teacher* won an Oscar for Best Documentary.

"The field of animal behavior," she said, "I don't think has ever been so exciting, because finally science has been forced to admit that we are part of the amazing animal kingdom, and it's not only us who have personalities, minds, and emotions. Now we're learning about the intelligence not just of chimpanzees and dolphins and elephants, but birds—there's a flurry of interest in avian intelligence—octopuses, even insects. And now we find trees can communicate with pheromones and microfungi under the roots on the forest floor. It's really an exciting time for young people wanting to go into this field."

That is her ultimate source of hope—the young people she has met through the years, primarily through Roots and Shoots, who remain a major focus of her work—this new generation armed with the knowledge to be better stewards than her own. She believes we are in a race against time. Climate change is real. Natural habitats continue to shrink. Extinction stalks the chimpanzee. And so there is no time for her to waste—no slowing down as long as her energy somehow remains, not even in the shadow of her ninetieth birthday. But there are those moments at her home in England, or her other one in Dar es Salaam, when she treasures the hours of reflection and quiet. Somebody asked in one of those times if there are still things she looks forward to, new adventures that might lie ahead.

"Dying," she replied.

She smiled to let the answer sink in, then continued, "If you think about it, there is either nothing, in which case, fine, it's over, you don't know anymore, why worry about it? Or there is something. And if there is, what greater adventure can there be?"

This idea, she said, was not entirely new in her life, or at least it was rooted in an earlier time. From the moment she arrived in the African forest, just a girl in pursuit of her dream, she had "the very strong feeling of a great spiritual power . . . the kind I've experienced in one of those old cathedrals in Europe where people have come to worship year after year." But in the forest, she said, that spiritual force became a great and powerful mystery, not something to set human beings apart but to bind them inevitably to all living things.

This, in the end, was the meaning of her work, the legacy and the truth she was seeking to impart through the lives she touched along the way.

In 2018, when my wife Nancy died of leukemia, I thought a lot about Jane Goodall—about wisdom and grace and the gentle example of lives well lived . . . and then, more personally, about the great shared privilege of shaking her hand.

The Bayou Doctor

After Hurricane Katrina made its catastrophic landfall in 2005, visiting death and devastation on the city of New Orleans, I wrote a series of stories about the forgotten eastern edge of that wreckage. These were published in the *Journal of American History*, and two anthologies, one of them from Oxford University Press, the other from NewSouth Books, where this particular piece appeared. With Sheila Hagler and Peggy Denniston, two artists who worked on the Alabama coast, I wrote and edited another book published by the University of Alabama Press. And finally, after the BP oil spill ravaged the Gulf of Mexico five years later, I returned again to this star-crossed community—and to the issue of environmental justice—on assignment for *Vanderbilt Magazine*. I tried to celebrate both the beauty and the difficulty of life in this place—all of the intricate issues it raised, and all of the humanity it evoked.

In the days just after Hurricane Katrina, the people of Bayou La Batre, Alabama—those who had lost everything in the storm—crowded together in a local auditorium, sleeping on cots, eating the meals that were provided twice a day. Already, volunteers were pouring into this tiny fishing village on the Alabama coast, where a battered population of twenty-three hundred souls extracted their modest living from the sea. They had lived through their share of hurricanes before, but never anything like this, never a storm surge of fifteen feet sweeping away everything in its path.

The people of the Bayou were reeling.

On the auditorium stage, a local doctor had set up shop, tending to the maladies of the hour—the cuts and bruises of the early cleanup, infections acquired from contaminated water, asthma and allergies from the mold-infested homes. As she went about her work, it didn't take long before the volunteers noticed something extraordinary about the doctor, a round-faced woman with soft, dark eyes and a radiant smile, and a manner that seemed both gentle and direct. Regina Benjamin was African American, but her patients were diverse—Black, white, and Asian—most of them from working-class families.

In 1990, Benjamin had opened her own health clinic on the Bayou, and in many ways it was a homecoming. She was raised on the shores of Mobile Bay, in the little town of Daphne maybe forty miles away, and she loved the easy rhythms of the coast—the subtle sunsets and changing color of the water and the way the people would look you in the eye. "These are warm-hearted people," she said, "and there is no pretense. They love you or they hate you."

In many ways, she decided, they were like the people in a lot of Southern towns—down-to-earth, hardworking—but in Bayou La Batre there was also a difference. The village was old by the standards of America, going back all the way to the 1700s, when French explorers sailed into the Gulf and began building settlements from the Mississippi River to Mobile Bay. In the middle of the eighteenth century, they placed a battery of cannons at the mouth of a bayou just west of Mobile, and the area became known as Bayou La Batre. A Frenchman named Joseph Bosarge applied for a grant of more than twelve hundred acres on the swampy western shore of the bayou, and his descendants today are scattered up and down that part of the coast.

For more than two centuries, they have shrimped or fished, or helped build the boats for the people who do, and their oral history has been a living thing. Until his death in the spring of 2007, Floyd Bosarge, one of Joseph's fifth-generation descendants, held a fish fry every Monday afternoon in a boat-building shed out behind his house. His friends and family members would gather, as they had every Monday for more than forty years, swapping stories and memories of life on the Bayou. Some of the tales were irreverent and funny, while others shaded from legend into myth, and all of them celebrated life with the sea.

"We love it like a farmer loves digging in the dirt," said longtime oysterman Avery Bates. "You're feeding your family and the people around you. You know you're involved in something worthwhile."

But if tradition runs deep in Bayou La Batre, it has been, for much of the current generation, an area bombarded by the forces of change. Almost certainly, the most dramatic change took shape in the 1970s when the war in Vietnam limped to an end and a stream of refugees from Southeast Asia—Laos, Cambodia, and Vietnam—began seeking sanctuary in the Bayou. Many arrived with memories nearly too gruesome to bear, stories they most often kept to themselves, of children gunned down by the Khmer Rouge or days they had spent at sea in leaky boats, trying to escape from Vietnam.

In Bayou La Batre, they quickly found work in the seafood shops, shucking oysters and cleaning crabs, and some eventually managed to buy their own boats, pursuing a life not altogether different from the one they had known in Southeast Asia. By the end of twentieth century, they made up a third of the local population, and for the refugees and the white and Black families who were now their neighbors, the adjustment did not come easily at first. There were scattered racial slurs in the schools, verbal confrontations among many of the shrimpers, and a few white families simply moved away.

And yet whatever the undertow of mistrust, when Regina Benjamin came to the Bayou she saw fundamental reasons for hope. Despite the barriers of language and culture—and the Asians wanted to hold on to what they could—she could see the beginnings of a mutual respect. In the crab and oyster shops, the refugees' work ethic was beyond reproach, and as one old salt from the Bayou put it, "It made Bayou La Batre even more of a seafood production town. The Asian workers would pick a hundred to a hundred and twenty pounds of crabmeat a day. They doubled the production of American pickers. If they were shucking oysters, they sometimes worked twelve hours a day, and changed the whole complexion of oyster production. They shrimped also. They bought up old boats and worked hard and upgraded their boats. They were heavy producers, and people had to respect that about them."

By 2005, when Hurricane Katrina headed for the coast, Dr. Benjamin, among many others, saw in the live-and-let-live world of the Bayou a reproach to the curious xenophobia that was sweeping through the country—the new epidemic of national disdain for the refugees from Mexico and other places who were doing the work that no Americans wanted but who were making more than they could ever have hoped to at home. That hostility toward strangers had long since faded in Bayou La Batre, and particularly in the wake of the catastrophic storm, Benjamin saw people now pulling together—white, Black, and Asian—in the uncertain struggle to rebuild the town.

Even in the middle of the hurricane itself, as the wind and water roared in from the Gulf, there were stories of color-blind heroism—of neighbors who turned to each other for survival. Sophol and Chandara

Ngam, refugees who worked in the seafood shops, remembered the steady rise of the flood, filling their house, and still it wouldn't stop. They waded outside as the water kept coming, kept getting deeper, and they knew that soon they would have to swim. But they didn't know how, and neither did most of their seven children. They began to call out, "No can swim! No can swim!" and finally Ralph Harbison, a volunteer fireman who lived nearby, appeared with a boat. As the whole Ngam family scrambled on board, Harbison waded through the chest-deep water and pulled them to safety.

"All I could think of," he told a reporter for the *Mobile Register*, "was getting them out of there."

It was a story repeated many times in the storm and the difficult period of recovery that followed. "There's still room for improvement," says Dr. Benjamin, "but there's been a lot of sharing in a small-town way. If somebody needed help during the storm, they didn't stay within their own group. People helped each other regardless. They knew that we are all in the same state."

If that realization, more and more, had become the new reality in the Bayou, most people said that Regina Benjamin was a part of the change. From the beginning, she was a reassuring presence with her cheerful smile, the crisp white coats that she wore in her office, and her manner of quiet and steady self-possession. She came to the village in 1990 and opened her storefront clinic near the water, and the word quickly spread among the people of the town that this doctor was different from many of her peers. The old-timers said she was like Mose Tapia, the family practitioner who served the community from the 1920s to the 1960s—in the days when doctors still made house calls. Working near the turn of the twenty-first century, Benjamin saw no reason why she shouldn't do the same. She would leave her office, which was, in fact, only a block or two from where Tapia's had been, and rumble through the town in her Toyota truck, dropping in on patients who couldn't come to her. Sometimes she would travel alone; other times she worked with Nell Bosarge Stoddard, her longtime nurse who was still going strong well into her seventies. Like the majority of people in Bayou La Batre, Nell Stoddard was white, but after a while nobody paid much attention to that—to the veteran nurse, who had lived in the Bayou for much of her life, working side by side with the young Black doctor who felt right at home.

"She loves this community," Stoddard later explained. "She's very down to earth. There's nothing about her that puts people off."

So they made their rounds and treated everybody who came through the door—shrimpers with shark bites, middle-aged women who had never had a Pap smear, shipyard workers with carpal tunnel syndrome. One day a deepwater shrimper came to the clinic after three weeks at sea, sporting an ugly gash on his hand. He said it had happened a few days earlier, and lacking any way to stitch it closed, he had poured peroxide into the wound, then superglued it shut. To Benjamin's amazement, it was healing just fine.

As the years went by, she found she loved these people on the Bayou, the hardworking men and their children and wives, who sometimes worked alongside the men on the boats, or in the crab shops, or shucking oysters hauled in from the bay. "The most calming time for me is talking to a patient," she said, and it never mattered what their backgrounds were. It was clear from the start that the blue-collar poor—who couldn't afford insurance but earned too much to qualify for Medicaid—deserved the same care as anybody else. And there were also patients who couldn't pay her at all, except perhaps with a bushel of oysters or homegrown pecans, or maybe five dollars at the end of the month. But she knew that all would pay what they could.

"These are proud people," she said. "They don't want charity."

In the early years, to supplement her clinic's meager revenues, Benjamin would work extra shifts in emergency rooms, or lecture sometimes to groups of physicians, and slowly but surely she began to develop a national reputation. *Reader's Digest* did a profile, and so did Rick Bragg of the *New York Times*, and on his national newscast for ABC, Peter Jennings chose Benjamin as his "Person of the Week." In 1998, she won the Nelson Mandela Award for Health and Human Rights, while serving on the board of the American Medical Association (the youngest doctor ever chosen to do so) and the Board of Physicians for Human Rights.

But her focus remained her clinic on the Bayou. She was caught in the struggles of the people in the town, particularly when the hurricanes came through, which began in earnest in 1998. On September 28, a dwindling storm called Georges hit the Mississippi coast, and the still-potent winds on the eastern side pushed a wall of water into Bayou La Batre. Benjamin's clinic was flooded, and her insurance paid only $20,000 toward replacing the building and everything that was in it. But she found a new site in the heart of downtown, took out a mortgage, and built a new clinic on four-foot stilts—the better to avoid future flood waters.

Hurricane Ivan hit the town in 2004, damaging homes and blowing down trees, and then came Katrina. The massive storm made its first landfall on August 25, 2005, as it crossed the southern tip of Florida and entered the warm and inviting waters of the Gulf. Over the next several days, it strengthened to Category 5, sending a storm swell surging toward the coast. On August 29, the wall of water swept through the Bayou, where the town existed essentially at sea level, and two thousand people were driven from their homes.

When the winds subsided, Benjamin drove over from Daphne to check on her clinic as well as her patients. When she arrived at her office, she thought at first that it didn't look too bad; the walls and the roof seemed to be intact, and she wondered if she had been lucky this time. But when she opened the door, she was hit with a stench that nearly made her sick. As *Reader's Digest* reported, "Seawater, old fish and dead crabs mingled with raw sewage. Chairs and tables were tossed about as if they'd been in a washing machine."

Benjamin and her nurse Nell Stoddard put on gloves and set out to salvage whatever they could, but they also knew that their patients were going to need them. In the chaotic week that followed the storm, they set up operations at the community center that doubled as a shelter. Grace Scire, one of the volunteers at the center, who later went to work in Benjamin's office, remembered the doctor with her reassuring smile ordering the medicines her patients had to have but couldn't afford after losing nearly everything in the storm. Insulin, antibiotics—whatever it was, Benjamin arranged for nearby pharmacists to fill the prescriptions and then send her the bills. She said she would pay them somehow.

"After the storm," Benjamin recalled, "we saw everybody for free for eight months. People didn't have their co-pays. But they needed care, and they needed their meds."

In Benjamin's mind, none of that was extraordinary, for it was part of a small-town way of life—distinctively Southern, some people might say—in which neighbors understood they were in it together. As a girl growing up on Mobile Bay, she had been raised on stories from the Great Depression—how her grandmother, a matriarch in Daphne's Black community, would put out lemonade and sandwiches for the hoboes passing by on the highway. Her mother played a similar role, and when Benjamin graduated from Xavier University in New Orleans and entered Morehouse School of Medicine, she developed her own caregiver's obsession with somehow making a difference. In 1982, she finished her degree at the University of Alabama at Birmingham, then spent her residency at a family practice clinic in Georgia before returning to the Alabama coast. "It was like coming home," she told one reporter. "I hope my patients get something because I get even more."

Most of the time she doesn't say much more, doesn't engage in public introspections about the basic motivations of her work. She is more likely to deflect questions with a joke. She once told a reporter from *People* magazine that in recruiting another doctor for her clinic, she would simply pass along what the job meant to her. The help-wanted ad, she said, might read: "Long hours, low pay, great job satisfaction and all the shrimp and oysters you can eat."

Embedded in the essential good humor of her comment is an admission that life in Bayou La Batre has been hard, especially in the two years following Katrina. In the difficult autumn of 2005, Benjamin mortgaged her home and maxed out her credit cards to restore and rebuild her clinic. It was set to reopen on January 2, 2006, when, incredibly, a fire broke out the night before and burned the modest new building to the ground. When Benjamin arrived and stared at the charred remains of her work, all she could think of, despite the first wave of depression and shock, was that she had to find a way to push ahead.

"We'll rebuild it," she told a reporter from the *Mobile Register*. "This will give me an opportunity to try and maybe do it differently. While I like what we had, maybe I can do it better."

And in fact, she did. She applied for federal money, and after sorting through the massive bureaucratic confusion, arranged for a grant of $1.1 million federal dollars routed through the state and then through Volunteers of America—to rebuild yet again. It was the kind of perseverance she saw all around her as the Bayou struggled against the odds to recover. And Katrina was not the community's only problem.

In the brave new world of a global economy, there were changes in the local seafood industry—an $80 million enterprise in the Bayou, which represented 85 percent of the area's economy. Perhaps most urgently, higher fuel prices and the competition from imported shrimp, now cheaper than those caught closer to home, were squeezing shrimpers' profit margins. "It's been just devastating," said Robert Shipp, professor of marine sciences at the University of South Alabama. "The future of the shrimp industry is not good at all."

Crabs and oysters have been more stable, but in Bayou La Batre, shrimp production has been the biggest industry, and to complicate matters, there has been an ongoing conflict between the shrimping fleet and commercial sports fishermen in pursuit of red snapper. The snapper are often caught in the shrimp nets, which has produced over time an intricate set of environmental regulations. Oystermen, too, have been embroiled in environmental debates. Mechanical dredging has recently been legalized, as it was in the middle of the twentieth century, and many oystermen fear that despite the efficiency of the dredging process, it will do major damage to the oyster beds.

In addition to all these uncertainties, there has been the specter of high-end development—big-money builders who have their eyes on the Bayou if the area can make it through a few more years without being struck by another hurricane. Many people are ambivalent about this new possibility. On the one hand, the economy needs a boost, and developers might be able to provide it. On the other hand, people are afraid that everything will change if suddenly new condos are lining the waterfront, bringing higher taxes and perhaps new pressure on old-timers to move. As one Alabama commentator put it, "The unanswered question, two years after the catastrophic storm, is whether the town can find the tricky balance between injecting new life and tearing out the old."

Regina Benjamin believes that it can, and she said she was happy to be a part of the attempt. For her part, she expects to expand her own clinic's work, hiring a physician's assistant and maybe two more doctors, and beginning a new cancer screening program to focus on the underserved parts of the community—particularly the Vietnamese. She knows that most of her patients are survivors, for indeed the whole community is that way—the whites, the Blacks, the Southeast Asians, and now the Mexican immigrants coming in. Together, they have made their way through the storms, and are battling through the economic hard times. And they also share a sense of common ground—a feeling of community—in this battered, multicultural New South village with old-fashioned values springing from its core.

Somehow there is hope in that simple truth, and as Benjamin put it in a recent interview, "There's nowhere else that I'd rather be."

Footnote: In the Path of the Oil

> In 2010, I wrote this article for *Vanderbilt Magazine,* and a shorter piece for the literary journal, *The Oracle,* about the disaster that followed Hurricane Katrina.

In Bayou La Batre, maybe ten miles from where I now live, the old-timers like to tell stories of the storms. These are mostly unembellished tales, some of them handed down for generations, about hurricanes roaring in from the Gulf. Nancy McCall, a veteran community activist in the Bayou, remembers growing up in a Baptist church where the minister, Will Prichard, would preach sometimes about a vision that came when he was still young.

It was just before the storm of 1906, and God appeared to Prichard in a dream, telling him he needed to move from his home. The preacher obeyed, and when the winds came ashore a few weeks later, the tidal surge from the deadly hurricane swept away the house in which he had lived. The worst part was that others didn't get the warning, and the image that stayed with Prichard through the years was of mothers and babies in the tops of pine trees. Some were alive, clinging to the limbs that saved them from the flood, while others had drowned, their bodies now wedged between the branches.

"He would cry, even in the pulpit, when he told that story," says Nancy McCall. "He could never get that picture from his mind."

Such stories are a staple all across the Gulf Coast, a place where residents freely acknowledge that life on the edge of the continent is hard. But there's a different feeling in the air these days. The old-timers will tell you that the hurricanes come and the hurricanes go, requiring resilience of those who survive. Now, however, there's the BP oil spill, by far the worst in U.S. history, and for all of us living here on the water, there is a fear of devastation that could last for decades. "It's like a monster that's out there," says Bayou La Batre mayor Stan Wright.

For some of us, the stakes are first of all aesthetic. We love the pelicans and the great blue herons, the cypress trees and the white sand beaches, and that haunting, subtle beauty of the marsh. Now, suddenly, the images of oil-soaked birds and deep red stains in the sawgrass savannah are themselves enough to break people's hearts. But the damage, of course, goes deeper than that. Bob Shipp, a marine biologist at the University of South Alabama where I teach, has spent his career studying both the ecosystem and the coastal way of life it supports. He knows the shrimpers and charter boat captains, the oystermen and blue-collar families in the seafood shops, and as the oil slick spreads across the northern Gulf, he is not optimistic about their future.

There is, most immediately, the killing of the animals—the fish and shrimp, oysters and crabs—that remain at the heart of the coastal way of life. Almost certainly, there are bad times ahead. But the deeper worry for Shipp and other scientists has to do with the habitat, the estuaries, and coastal marshes where 80 percent of the marine species spend at least part of their lives. "If the oil coats the sea-grass blades," says Shipp, "it'll do some damage, but the grass will snap back. But if it gets in the sediment and kills the roots, then it will be years."

There is also the deepwater counterpart to the marsh. Some twenty miles or more offshore, vast beds of sargassum, or floating seaweed, serve as a nursery for the eggs and juveniles of more than a hundred species of fish. With the oil slick already lapping at the marsh and drifting inexorably toward the seaweed, the potential for long-term damage is vast—made worse, many say, by BP's massive use of dispersants.

Immediately after the April explosion that killed eleven workers and unleashed a gusher five thousand feet below the surface, the company began to spray Corexit, a toxic chemical that breaks up the oil and causes it to sink. In early May, Shipp and fellow scientist George Crozier, director of the Dauphin Island Sea Lab, met with BP officials to argue against the use of the dispersant. The meeting did not go well. The BP scientists, as Shipp later told the *Mobile Press-Register*, didn't want to hear about the dangers of sunken oil or the long-term threat to the Gulf's food chain. "When we started talking about the sediments and the food web," Shipp said, "they just turned off."

With such stories making their rounds on the coast, there is, as I sit down to write, a palpable intermingling of anger and despair. In Louisiana, where the damage so far has been the worst, people often struggle to put it into words. "You can't sleep no more, that's how bad it is," John Blanchard, an oyster fisherman, told Bob Herbert of the *New York Times*. "My wife and I have got two kids, 2 and 7. We could lose everything we've been working all of our lives for."

What Blanchard and others find hard to explain is that they have been part of an ancient bargain, dating back as long as people can remember. Avery Bates, an oysterman in Bayou La Batre who saw his community devastated by Katrina, then slowly rebuild, was, like many of his neighbors, he says, sustained by the fundamental logic of what he was doing. As Bates understood it, the bounty of the sea was always there, offering a good and honorable living, with rewards that were roughly equal to your work.

"You're part of a heritage going back for generations," says Bates. "You sweat hard, but you know why you do it. You're feeding your family and the people around you. You know you're a part of something worthwhile."

But now many people on the Gulf Coast believe something fundamental has been lost. They know the story of Prince William Sound—how the oil that spilled from the *Exxon Valdez* killed off whole populations of herring, and how, more than twenty years later, thousands of gallons can still be found in the coastal sediments of Alaska. And today on the Gulf, even the old-timers who are used to the struggle—the summer hurricanes, the seasons when the harvests are thinner than normal—say they don't know what will happen next.

"This whole thing could shut us down," says Billy Parks, who runs a seafood shop in Bon Secour, Ala. "I've been here for 35 years selling seafood fresh out of the Bay and Gulf. My grandfather did it before me and then my dad. I could get frozen, imported seafood and sell it, but that's not what I do. They're out there trying to make billions of dollars a year, and they put us all at risk. I'm praying and trusting God to take care of us, and I believe he will. I put it in his hands. If it puts us out of business, I'll do something. I don't know what, but something."

For Parks and many others, that's all that seems to be left at the moment . . . some hybrid of fatalism and faith, as the poisonous scar of BP oil spreads slowly, inevitably across the Gulf.

Epilogue

After more than ten years, the aftermath was still unclear. "A decade later," wrote the editors at *National Geographic*, "many species, such as deep-sea coral, common loons, and spotted sea trout, are still struggling, their populations lower than before. By contrast, a few Gulf inhabitants have shown a robust recovery—among them, menhaden fish, and the brown pelican. . . . Scientists say it's still too early to tell definitely what the impact has been for longer-lived species such as dolphins, whales, and sea turtles." Meanwhile, activist organizations along on the Coast, including Mobile Bay Keeper, worry about other potential disasters, including Alabama Power Company's decision to store twenty-one million pounds of coal ash on the banks of the Mobile River.

In his book *Saving America's Amazon*, award-winning environmental reporter Ben Raines describes a delicate ecosystem still under siege. "We are not nearly so good," he concludes, "at protecting air and water, people and wild animals from the caustic effects of industry and development as most of us would like to believe."

He hopes this dismal reality will change. He also knows that it's an uphill climb.

Songs of the South

Singer-songwriters have been a recurring fascination, and I have tended to regard them first through the lens of literature—as writers reflecting on the human condition. The next four stories are about some of my favorite performers. All of them are, or were, based in Nashville, where, despite the wretched state of commercial country music, there are still artists committed to the craft. The profiles of Kathy Mattea and Matraca Berg were first published in *Americana Gazette*. The story of songwriter Peter Cooper and baseball legend Hank Aaron was written for the book page of the *Mobile Press Register*, and the story of DeFord Bailey, the first African American star in country music, and his biographer, David Morton, was published in the online journal *Chapter 16*.

Coal
The West Virginia Roots of a Country Star

Kathy Mattea is sitting quietly at her kitchen table in Nashville, reflecting on the recent change in her career. She remembers the precise and painful moment when she knew she would take this unexpected dive, this shift in focus from commercial country music to the sweet and sorrowful sounds of Appalachia. Actually, as some who followed her music might argue, the change was not—lyrically at least—quite as dramatic as it appeared. But with two new albums, the Grammy-nominated *Coal*, released in 2008, and the even more personal *Calling Me Home*, coming four years later, Mattea's music was now fully tied to the "reluctant activism" that had tugged at her heart for twenty years.

The turning point came in a moment of horror. On January 2, 2006, a coal mine exploded in Sago, West Virginia, a hill-country town about a hundred miles northeast of Charleston. Carbon monoxide flooded the hole, making it nearly impossible to breathe, as grief-stricken families gathered in a tiny Baptist church only a few hundred yards from the mine. Then, improbably, just before midnight, word of a miracle reached the church. Rescuers had discovered one body, but twelve other miners were said to be alive.

"The church bells ring and people pour out rejoicing," reported Frank Langfitt of National Public Radio. "Reporters at the scene beam the story around the globe, 'Miracle in the hills of West Virginia.'"

But then just as suddenly, around 3:00 a.m., company officials came to the church, looking grim-faced, maybe even afraid. Sadly, they said, reports of a miracle had been wrong. Only one miner had managed to survive. Twelve others were dead, apparently from breathing the poisonous air. Cries of anger erupted in the church, shouts of "Liar!" as the officials quickly retreated from the crowd. For many of the people in the church that night, this was West Virginia in microcosm—a place of stark and endless contradiction, of beauty and strength, but also of exploitation and death, of indifference and greed and a callous disregard for the people and the land.

Kathy Mattea was surprised at first by the force with which she felt these things. A native West Virginian, she listened to reports coming out of Sago, sharing at first in the soaring hopes that were swept away so completely by the sadness and rage. "I was feeling a grief that shocked me," she remembers. "I burst into tears in the middle of the afternoon." And soon her connection became more direct. The news show *Larry King Live* covered the funeral on CNN, and Mattea was asked to provide a song to close out the broadcast. She chose one of her own, a mournful ballad that she had cowritten, and the heartbreak of it was nearly unbearable as she sang her epitaph for the miners:

> The memory of the smile, the tear
> The slender threads that bind us here.

Nearly seven years later, at her home in Nashville, she remembered how, soon after that, an irresistible notion began to take hold, even though she tried to fight it at first. "For years," she explained, "I had had an idea in my head about some kind of record about home or the mountains or Appalachia or something. But after the Sago disaster, I thought, 'I need to do an album about coal.' I didn't want to. It was like, 'No, no, not coal-mining. It's going to be depressing. It's going to be twangy.' I had a few songs squirreled away, like 'Dark as a Dungeon' by Merle Travis, and 'Coal Tattoo,' by Billy Edd Wheeler, who was also a native West Virginian. So, reluctantly, I began to search for other coal-mining songs."

One of those she discovered early on was "Lawrence Jones," written by a Southern folk singer by the name of Si Kahn, who was soon to become one of her closest friends. Kahn, a community organizer as well as a songwriter, had worked in 1973 on the Brookside strike in eastern Kentucky. For more than a year, as the chilly winds blew through Harlan County, the coal miners walked the picket lines, trying to secure a contract with Duke Power Company, the owner of the Brookside mine. For more than a year, Duke Power resisted, determined to drive the United Mine Workers Union from the company's mines. The standoff grew increasingly bitter, increasingly violent, until finally a young miner named Lawrence Jones was shot in the face in an early morning clash. He died soon after, leaving behind a teenage wife and a baby, and only then did the company finally come to the table.

Kahn wrote a song in memory of Jones, and it became a centerpiece of Kathy Mattea's new album, *Coal*. And there were others, reflecting the deep ambivalence with which many people in southern Appalachia now regard their greatest natural resource. In his iconic "Dark as a Dungeon," Merle Travis put the feeling this way:

> Like a fiend with his dope and a drunkard his wine
> A man will have lust for the lure of the mine.

When Kahn heard Mattea sing that song, as well as his own, he was impressed, as most people are, by the beauty of her voice. But he also thought he heard something more—a depth of conviction—confirmed when he met her in Charlotte, North Carolina, not long after the release of her album.

"We met backstage after one of her shows," Kahn remembers.

> We traded CDs, and I loved her version of "Lawrence Jones." This was a young man who was shot for no reason—and *for a reason*—because Duke Power wanted to control their own coal. Kathy is very people-oriented. She has a big heart, and she hates violence of any kind. I think she felt a moral call leading up to this album, this new direction in her career, and you can hear it in every one of her songs. I've heard her refer to herself as a "recovering country music star," which is funny and a great reflection of her sense of humor. But it also has several different layers. There's self-deprecation, maybe a little bit of regret because she's not on the country charts anymore. But there's also a strong sense of purpose.

Carefully, trying not to sound self-important, Mattea tends to agree with that assessment. "I feel like these last two albums are part of what I'm supposed to be doing," she explains.

> I grew up in West Virginia, where both my grandfathers had been *coal* miners, and the more I listened, the more this music rang true to me. Overall, the synchronicity of my *Coal* album was so great that I felt like I was sitting in some kind of rocket ship. My biggest fear was that most of these songs were not written for commercial purposes, and I was worried that having grown up in commercial music, I would sound smarmy. But somebody suggested Marty Stuart as producer. He understood this

kind of music . . . and when he said he would produce it, I relaxed. I knew he would serve the music first. We used nothing but Appalachian instruments, except for a cello on Billy Edd Wheeler's "Coming of the Roads," and a little bit of piano in one other place. We tried to make it as organic as it could be.

And yet, it's also true that whatever its anticommercial intent, *Coal* enjoyed a clear measure of success. Perhaps because of its very boldness—the decision, for example, to close the album with maybe the most depressing coal song of all time, the heartfelt Hazel Dickens dirge "Black Lung"—Mattea's *Coal* was nominated for a Grammy as the best folk album of 2008.

I still remember the first time I heard it. I was struck initially, as most people are, by how deliberately uncommercial it sounded, with its banjos and high lonesome fiddles and even a few moments of pure a cappella. But the more I listened, the more it seemed that this was fundamentally an extension—much more that than a departure—of the music Mattea had made all along. Her career in Nashville had come together around the records she made with Allen Reynolds, a producer who always seemed more at home with the folk music side of the Nashville sound. Reynolds had enjoyed great success with artists such as Don Williams, Garth Brooks, and Crystal Gayle, and he and Mattea proved to be a good fit.

On her 1986 album *Walk the Way the Wind Blows*, produced by Reynolds, Mattea had her first major hit, a Nanci Griffith song called "Love at the Five and Dime." To Mattea the song was like finding a literary gem—"a lifetime in three minutes," as she later put it. "All the big life moments are covered." Somehow it seemed appropriate that Griffith, when Mattea met her back in those days, always seemed to have her nose in a book, often something by the great Southern writer Eudora Welty.

Thus did an affinity for music as *story* become a trademark of Mattea's career. Her string of hits included "Eighteen Wheels and a Dozen Roses" about a truck-driving man who was ready to retire and spend time with his wife, and "She Came from Ft. Worth" about a Texas waitress with a heart full of dreams who runs away with one of her customers to a cabin in the Colorado Rockies. And perhaps more powerfully than any of the others, there was the Grammy-winning song "Where Have You Been?" cowritten by her husband, Jon Vezner. It's about a love that endures through every phase of life, even the final stages of dementia, when an old woman lies alone in her hospital bed and a nurse brings her husband to her room in a wheelchair.

Given her love of those kinds of songs—*folk songs*, really, that tell a human story—it should have come as no surprise that Mattea would be drawn to the songs of Appalachia. For one thing, this was her *place*, the heart of her cultural DNA, and she knew that *Coal* would not be her last attempt to explore that connection. As she began recording *Calling Me Home*, released in the summer of 2012, she felt as if she were digging even deeper in the same fertile soil. Perhaps it was because she had gotten to know the legendary Appalachian writers—people like Jean Ritchie and Hazel Dickens—whose songs she was now beginning to sing.

She first met Ritchie at the Philadelphia Folk Festival, and on that occasion and others Mattea found herself, as she put it later, "sitting at her feet and asking her questions." But if Mattea at first was a little awestruck (a state of mind that is not her style), it was clear right away that Jean Ritchie was not. She regarded Mattea not as a country music star but simply as a fellow singer of songs. Ritchie, a Kentucky native still performing at the age of ninety, was the youngest of fourteen children born on a Cumberland Mountain farm. In 1946, she graduated from the University of Kentucky and moved soon after to New York City, where she began hanging out with such folk-singing legends as Pete Seeger, Leadbelly, and Woody Guthrie. A skilled musician in her own right, she played the dulcimer and became known over time as "The Mother of Folk," writing her share of iconic songs.

Kathy Mattea has added several of those songs to her standard repertoire, including "Black Waters," which is, on its face, a protest song against strip-mining.

> The hillside explodes with the dynamite's roar
> And the voice of the small bird is heard there no more
> Then the mountain comes tumbling so awful and grand
> And the poison black waters run down through my land.

The thing, however, that drew Mattea to the song and made it fit so perfectly into *Calling Me Home* was that it was so much more than a ballad of protest. In the largest sense it was a song about life—about an Appalachian farmer's love of the land, and the cycles of sadness that weave their way through the ordinary joys.

In the coming of springtime we planted our corn
In the ending of springtime we buried a son.

Mattea says her conversations with Ritchie have deepened her feeling about such songs, cementing the sense of a legacy that needs to be preserved. Once backstage a few years ago, when Ritchie was performing periodically but starting to feel the weight of the years, she told Mattea, "I can't get around like I used to. I can't get out and play as much."

"That's okay," Mattea told her, "we'll keep singing your songs. You rest now. We'll carry the torch."

She feels the same way about other folk legends she has met in recent years, people such as Alice Gerrard, whose ballad "Agate Hill" is one of the most beautiful cuts on *Calling Me Home*. And she may have felt an even closer kinship to her fellow West Virginian, Hazel Dickens. Dickens, who died in April 2011, was born in 1935 during the depths of the Depression and raised in poverty in the coal camps. Her father was a Primitive Baptist preacher, her brothers were miners, and one of her sisters cleaned house for the superintendent of the mines. As a young woman, Hazel moved from West Virginia to Baltimore, where she spent most of her life, but her heart and soul—and certainly her music—belonged to West Virginia.

In the 1960s, she and Alice Gerrard formed a bluegrass duo called Hazel and Alice. But Dickens's piercing solo laments, like her song "Black Lung," which she wrote in memory of her brother, are clearly at the heart of her legacy. She sang her songs for the people back home, sometimes taking her place on picket lines, and defined herself and an activist much more than simply an entertainer.

"I had met Hazel in passing," says Mattea, "but my first real encounter was in 2008 when we inducted her into the first class of the West Virginia Music Hall of Fame. Allison Krauss did the introduction of her. Then at the Folk Alliance in Memphis in 2009, I got to interview her in front of an audience. She had lived her life as an expatriate, having left West Virginia physically, but it was the lens through which she viewed everything. Unlike Jean Ritchie, Hazel did not have the same formal education, so there was no filter. There was such a directness that you find in Appalachia in the rural places, this combination of innocence and fierceness.

"I told her that learning to sing 'Black Lung' changed the way I think about singing. She just looked at me and paused and told me the story of her brother having black lung. She would not engage on the level of 'kiss my ring.' That's not who she was."

Many of Mattea's friends see some of those same qualities in Kathy, the same lack of pretension, the same sense of place, tender and fierce, embodied by Dickens and her peers. "I've known for some time," writes best-selling author Barbara Kingsolver, herself a native of Appalachian Virginia, "that Kathy is no stranger to that kind of gumption." Kingsolver and Mattea have developed a friendship in recent years through the crusade against mountaintop removal, a modern technique—strip-mining on steroids—that continues to rain devastation on the mountains.

"The particular genius of Kathy Mattea," Kingsolver wrote in the liner notes of *Calling Me Home*, "is to call up the touchstones of hope and heartache ... where you feel a little torn up because no matter which way you're headed, you are going towards home and also leaving it behind. Believe me, this is the soundtrack for that journey."

For Mattea, meanwhile, it seems clear enough that never in the course of her long career has the journey been richer than it is today.

The Dreaming Fields of Matraca Berg

For a decade or more, as she pursued her career as a Hall of Fame songwriter, Matraca Berg thought she might never make another record. Or at least if she did, she finally decided, it would be the album that *she* wanted to make. Meanwhile, the songs kept coming, springing from a dark and complicated place, the melodies sad, the lyrics shot through with longing and loss. But she found a measure of beauty in that, a redemption of sorts as she wrote the stories of her family and her life.

There was, for example, "The Dreaming Fields," telling the story of a Wisconsin farm that held the memories of her childhood summers, and even her teenage loss of innocence. And there was also "Oh, Cumberland," which began to take shape sometime early in the 1990s, when she was trying to make a record in California and was caught in the snarl of an LA freeway. As Merle Haggard sang "Big City" on her car radio, Matraca found herself weeping from the sadness of it all, that feeling she had of being out of place and wanting simply to go back home.

Raised in Nashville, with family roots in Kentucky and Wisconsin, Berg was born to the songwriter's life. Musicians were everywhere in her family. Her aunt, Sudie Callaway, was a successful backup singer in Nashville, and her uncle, Jim Baker, played steel guitar and ran Mel Tillis's publishing company. And back in Kentucky, two more of her relatives—Colleida Callaway and Clara Howard—were regulars on the Renfro Valley Barn Dance.

"They sang like angels," Matraca remembers.

But almost certainly it was her mother, Icie Berg, who supplied the earliest inspiration for her art. Icie was a native of Harlan County, Kentucky, "Bloody Harlan," as it was known in history, where deadly labor strikes in the 1930s, and again in the early 1970s, had inspired a legacy of musical protest. The legendary Aunt Molly Jackson, a folk icon of the Great Depression, sang with eloquent, unmistakable rage about the brutality inflicted on Harlan County miners.

It was, however, pain of a much more personal kind that drove Matraca's mother from the scarred hillsides of her Harlan County home. In 1964, as a pregnant teenager, she set off alone for Nashville, determined to make her mark as a singer. She never did. Instead, she took a job as a nurse and set about raising her brown-eyed daughter, who seemed early on to have the songwriter's gift. Matraca wrote her first hit at the age of eighteen, and Icie wept with a mixture of gentle envy and pride.

A year later she was dead, the victim of lymphoma at the age of forty, and for Matraca the pain never quite went away. It seemed, instead, to color and deepen her understanding of life, the melancholy of a young poet's heart, and even today you can hear it in her songs. Certainly, it is there in *The Dreaming Fields*, her CD released in 2011. This is Berg at her best—a powerful collection of Americana music, built around memories of a Wisconsin farm, and a river that flows through her home in Tennessee.

"I made this record with many of my closest friends," she says, "after being out of the recording business for nearly thirteen years. This was the only way I could have done it."

Berg has always worked closely with her friends, cowriting most of her major songs. It was a habit that began when she met Bobby Braddock, one of Nashville's most successful songwriters, recently inducted into the Country Music Hall of Fame. She was just a teenager at the time, writing a few songs, often with coaching help from her mother. Through her family connections, she had met a couple of Nashville's finest—Red Lane, who had written "Til I Get It Right" for Tammy Wynette and "New Looks from an Old Lover" for B. J. Thomas; and Sonny Throckmorton, who had written for Emmylou Harris, the Oak Ridge Boys, and Jerry Lee Lewis.

"I was hanging out at Tree Publishing," Matraca remembers.

> I felt good about going over there. We were passing the guitar around one day, and I played something and Bobby Braddock said, "Do you know how good that is?" This was the guy who had written "D-I-V-O-R-C-E," so later that summer a group of us young writers, who followed him around like puppy dogs, were over at his house. I was playing his piano and he sat down, and together we wrote "Faking Love" in about twenty minutes.

In 1983, it went to number one for T. G. Sheppard and Karen Brooks. I was eighteen. I thought, "Oh, no, I'm not ready for this."

About that time, she joined a Top 40 band in Louisiana—"I fell for the keyboard player," she explains—and for the next little while she wrote what she calls "a lot of mediocre pop songs." But then her mother got sick, and when Icie Berg died in 1984, it was, for Matraca, like losing a best friend—an "all-encompassing" kind of grief that, among other things, left her with a whole different feeling about songs.

"I got serious after that," she says. "I started trying a little harder."

In 1987, Reba McEntire hit number one with Matraca's "Last One to Know," and over the next several years some of the biggest stars in country music—Tanya Tucker, Ray Price, and Randy Travis—began to turn to Berg for material. With her visibility on the rise, she cut her first album in 1990, but the release of *Lying to the Moon* ushered in a double-edged time in her career. Two singles from the record made the country charts, but her label, RCA, saw Matraca as a pop singer, and the album that followed, *The Speed of Grace*, fell into an artistic no-man's-land. "It was neither fish, nor fowl," she says, and in her disillusionment with the process, Matraca waited four years to make another record.

Even then, the results were disheartening. Measured by its artistry alone *Sunday Morning to Saturday Night* was a brilliant piece of work. Released in 1997 on Rising Tide Records, it contained one of Berg's most memorable songs, "Back When We Were Beautiful," a haunting ballad about a woman growing old:

> I guess you had to be there, she said, you had to be
> She handed me a yellow photograph and then said, see
> This was my greatest love, my one and only love and this is me
> Back when we were beautiful, see.

It was a magical moment when Matraca sang the song at the CMA Awards, and for people who were there it was hard to imagine that she wouldn't be a star. She looked so beautiful, for one thing, with her long brown hair and large, dark eyes and the trace of a smile both confident and shy. But it was her voice that people remembered that night, so silky and strong and so full of heart.

"Matraca Berg nearly stole the CMA Awards," declared *Entertainment Weekly*. But her song never made the country charts, for almost as soon as the album was released, Rising Tide Records went bankrupt. "I definitely wondered about my record karma," she says looking back. "I also felt like maybe you get signals you are barking up the wrong tree."

But if she grew ambivalent about recording, she was more and more committed to the art of writing songs. And on that front there was no ambiguity about her success. The string of number ones that began in the eighties continued through the nineties with songs like "Hey, Cinderella" that she wrote with Suzy Bogguss and "Wrong Side of Memphis" that she wrote for Trisha Yearwood.

Measured commercially, or even by its critical acclaim, her biggest hit came in 1997. Nashville artist Deanna Carter, for her debut release, chose Matraca's "Strawberry Wine," one of the most personal songs that she ever wrote. It's a steamy ballad of teenage love, and the story it tells is mostly her own:

> He was working through college on my grandpa's farm.
> I was thirsting for knowledge and he had a car.

The song is set on a Wisconsin farm, the family homestead of her adoptive father, Ron Berg, where Matraca often spent her summers as a child. Dairy cattle grazed on the rolling hillsides, and corn grew tall in the cool summer breeze, and the warmth and love of extended family left a deep imprint on her songs. The same was true of her roots in Kentucky, the hills and hollows near the village of Wallins, where her family had lived since the days of Daniel Boone, and where at the age of twelve she would play piano at her grandmother's church.

Songs such as "Appalachian Rain," which she recorded with Emmylou Harris, and "Strawberry Wine"—which, in addition to the obvious story of passion, speaks of the bittersweet passage of time—stamped Matraca in the estimation of her peers as a songwriter at the very top of her game. She won a CMA Award for "Strawberry Wine," has written eleven number one hits, and in 2008, at the age of forty-four, became one of the youngest members of the Nashville Songwriter's Hall of Fame.

"Matraca has the gift," says her friend and mentor Bobby Braddock, "and she's smart enough to know what to do with it."

But for all of her success in the songwriting realm, there was still the nagging pull of the studio, the feeling that she had never quite gotten it right. "I felt like I was an imposter," she says. But Suzy Bogguss and Gretchen Peters didn't see it that way. On recent tours of the United Kingdom, where the three singer-songwriters shared the stage, they urged Matraca to make a new record. She already had the material, they said, and Matraca had to agree that it was true.

With Gary Harrison she had written "Oh Cumberland" and "The Dreaming Fields," two songs that carried her back to her roots, and with Marshall Chapman, "Your Husband's Cheatin' on Us," based on a tongue-in-cheek short story by Jill McCorkle. But perhaps most powerfully, she had teamed with Troy Verges and Sharon Vaughn to write "South of Heaven," a song that began to take shape in her mind when her brother-in-law shipped off to Iraq. "His mother was coming apart," says Matraca. "She had this deep, heart-breaking fear in her eyes. She was pale all the time."

Berg had wanted to write about the war, not something preachy, but something human and real, and she began to think about her own mother's face when Icie's brother wrote home from Vietnam. "She just would not be right for three or four days." And finally, she says, there was the televised image of Cindy Sheehan, the antiwar activist who had lost her only son in Iraq. As Matraca was sitting down with her songwriting partners, a pair of lines welled up from somewhere deep in her memory—images of faith, perhaps from a wood-framed church in Kentucky, now put to the test by the tragedy of war.

> God, you gave your only son
> You were not the only one.

Believing in the songs, Matraca went to Dualtone, an independent label with a love of great writers, and together they decided to give it a go. The resulting CD, which they decided to call *The Dreaming Fields*, is a powerful body of Americana music, delivered in Matraca's silky, unmistakable voice. There are songs of sadness and songs of hurt, but all of them carry the redemption of beauty and the clarity and heart of a poet looking back.

"Matraca is beautiful and writes beautifully," says her songwriting friend Marshall Chapman. "Her songs are artful, yet accessible. She digs deep for that heart of gold, yet she can put you back in the saddle, baby, yeah, stand you up tall."

Berg herself is a little more restrained, unaccustomed as she is to heaping praise on herself. But she has to admit when you ask about the album, "I'm pretty darn happy with the way it turned out."

715

A Baseball Legend in a Country Song

> On the thirty-fifth anniversary of Henry Aaron's record-breaking home run, one of the great achievements in baseball history, I wrote this reflection for Aaron's hometown newspaper, the *Mobile Press Register*.

Not long ago, for an upcoming book on civil rights sites, I wrote an entry on Henry Aaron, who in a sense completed the journey that Jackie Robinson began. Thirty-five years ago, Aaron, the Hall of Famer from Mobile, Alabama, broke the home run record of Babe Ruth, receiving a flood of hate mail as he closed in steadily on 715. As the letters poured into his Atlanta Braves office, more than 60 percent of them were negative, and at least a few contained open threats. "Martin Luther King was a troublemaker and had a short life span," one writer declared. And another wrote more ominously, "My gun is watching your every black move."

It seems incredible from the vantage point of today that Aaron's achievement, carried out with such grace, could possibly have prompted an outpouring of hate. But that was America in the 1970s, a nation still raw from the danger and tension of the civil rights years. When the record finally fell, on April 8, 1974, Aaron's mother, Estella, rushed from the stands to meet her son at home plate—in part to share in the joy of the moment but also to offer herself as a shield in case an assassin was waiting in the stands.

Writing about all of this, I wanted to capture, as other authors have, the drama and poignancy of the moment. And to be quite honest, I thought I had done a pretty good job, holding my own with Aaron's biographers and assorted sports writers who have done their own brand of justice to the story.

But then I heard Peter Cooper's version. Cooper is a longtime friend of mine, a mild-mannered newspaperman by day who covers music for the *Tennessean* in Nashville. In many ways, it is Cooper's dream job. He has always been a lover of good music, treating it not only as escape or entertainment but also as source of good writing.

In the songs of Johnny Cash, Kris Kristofferson, and Tom T. Hall, Cooper says he found great American stories, and it occurred to him a few years ago that he should write a few songs of his own. One of the catalysts was his friend Todd Snider, a young songwriter from Portland, Oregon, now living in Nashville, who has amassed a kind of cult-figure following for the wit and originality of his music.

Three years ago, Cooper and Snider started touring together, and as Cooper began to perform his own songs, he decided to write one about Henry Aaron. As a little boy growing up in South Carolina, he had been an avid Atlanta Braves fan, and Aaron had been his favorite player. There was something about the fluid way he played, gliding after fly balls in the outfield, hitting searing line drives with just a crack of the wrists. The ball somehow would continue to rise, clearing the outfield fence, and Aaron would begin his home run jog—never celebratory or defiant, never calling undue attention to himself, just a ball player trying to do his job.

There were others who were much flashier—contemporaries such as Willie Mays or Mickey Mantle or even Aaron's fellow Mobilian, Willie McCovey, who hit his towering home run blasts against the fierce winds of Candlestick Park. But Cooper was drawn to the quiet superstar, and many years later when he learned the full story of 715—the death threats, the slurs and epithets coming daily in the mail—he began to appreciate Aaron even more.

Throughout the pursuit of Babe Ruth's record, Aaron had carried himself with such restraint, letting his bat do the talking as his friend Jackie Robinson had urged him to do. Aaron, like Robinson, was never afraid to speak out for civil rights, but he rarely complained about his own ordeal, noting simply in his frequent interviews that he would be glad when the whole thing was over.

When Cooper began to write this story, he came to Mobile to visit Aaron's old neighborhood in Toulminville. In many ways, it hadn't changed much. The signs of poverty were there all around, and when Cooper saw the sunbaked field just up the street from the Aaron home place, he could easily imagine a whole different time:

Jim Crow smilin' while the sun beat down
On a sandlot field on the wrong side of town.

Cooper also pored over newspaper files, and he came upon a story from 1957—Aaron's fourth year in the majors—about an Aaron home run winning the pennant for the Milwaukee Braves. Aaron, then twenty-three, was named the league's most valuable player, and the newspaper showed him in the arms of his teammates, celebrating their triumph, while below the fold there were reports of race riots in Little Rock, Arkansas.

In his song, titled "715," Cooper captured the moment this way:

He won the pennant for the Braves with a four-base knock
The same day they were rioting in Little Rock
Up in ole Milwaukee he was MVP
Back in Alabama he was still not free
Not free to drink a beer in the white folks' lounge
Not free to have a meal in Mobile downtown.

As he was writing that verse, Cooper called an old musical acquaintance, a Hall of Fame steel guitar player by the name of Lloyd Green, to ask about its authenticity. Cooper knew Green had grown up in Mobile and would have known the city well in its Jim Crow era. And when Green said, yeah, Cooper's verse had it right, Cooper asked him to play on the record.

The result is stunning—a country song, fully six and a half minutes long, about the stoic heroism of a Black baseball player. Musically, it's built around Green's pedal steel guitar and Cooper's easygoing tenor voice, but the power of it comes from the story it tells—the "truth and beauty," as the songwriter put it, that Aaron and his bat turned loose on the world.

When the song was released on Cooper's first compact disc, a critically acclaimed album called *Mission Door*, he didn't expect much airplay. The song, after all, was more than six minutes long. But satellite radio began to play it, and when Cooper was interviewed on the nationally syndicated *Bob Edwards Show*, the song that Edwards wanted to talk about most was the one about Aaron. "Even touring in Europe," Cooper remembered, "people in Germany and Holland were grooving on the song."

Looking back on it, Cooper isn't surprised. He understands that the history at the heart of Aaron's story goes far beyond the pursuit of Babe Ruth, or a number in the record books of baseball. Aaron's quest in the end was a rite of passage for the whole country—perhaps the last time anywhere in America that an athlete, simply because he was Black, would endure such open animosity and hatred.

The anniversary we celebrate is about Hank Aaron putting all that to rest. He did it quietly with a fierce combination of humility and pride, his ambition tempered with dignity and grace. As he himself would put it later on, he was mostly a man who came to work every day, and "played the game as it's supposed to be played."

Epilogue

In 2022, songwriter Peter Cooper died unexpectedly at the age of fifty-two. He left behind a wife and son whom he loved, and a professional legacy as a performer and one of the finest music journalist/historians ever to come through Nashville.

Reclaiming the Legacy of a Country Music Star

> In 1975, I had the good fortune to interview DeFord Bailey, the first African American star in country music, for an article in *Country Music* magazine. In 2023, in an essay for *Chapter 16*, I returned to the subject for a posthumous look at Bailey's legacy—and the people who have worked to preserve it.

On a warm summer day in 1983, an unlikely mixture of family and friends, flanked by reporters and television crews, gathered one last time to pay tribute to a man who had once been a country music legend.

To some, DeFord Bailey was a name long forgotten, but not to those who came this day, who understood his character and talent—a life that was, as one of them put it, "a parable of integrity and survival." In their recently rereleased biography, *DeFord Bailey: A Black Star in Early Country Music*, historians David C. Morton and Charles K. Wolfe described the cemetery scene this way: "One by one, the cars reached the main entrance and began to turn north. . . . In front of them was a monument draped in white cloth; behind them were the old trees and gentle hills of the back part of the cemetery. . . . The grounds sloped down to the tracks of the Louisville & Nashville Railroad—appropriate, perhaps, given the love of railroads by the man they had come to honor."

The people at the graveside, especially the musicians such as Bill Monroe and Roy Acuff, all understood that DeFord Bailey found his musical inspiration everywhere—in the Methodist churches he attended as a child, in the "Black hillbilly" tunes of his once enslaved, fiddle-playing grandfather, but also in the lonesome sound of a passing locomotive.

In 1927, on the night the Grand Ole Opry got its name, Bailey opened the show with a train song, "Pan American Blues," after radio announcer George D. Hay made the segue from NBC's Music Appreciation Hour. The network show had ended that night with a symphonic composition inspired by a train, and Hay was only too happy to draw a comparison. "For the past hour," he said, "we have been listening to music largely from Grand Opera, but from now on, we will present the Grand Ole Opry."

Bailey followed with his harmonica solo, "swooping in one phrase," wrote Morton and Wolfe, "from a loud, braying trainlike phrase to a gentle, fluttering arpeggio." Opry audiences were dazzled by his talent, and he quickly became one of the biggest stars in country music—"the Harmonica Wizard," as Hay often put it.

In his graveside tribute, Acuff, who joined the Opry cast in 1938 and soon became known as "the King of Country Music," remembered how in the early days he liked to perform with Bailey because he "could draw a crowd when nobody knew Roy Acuff." He called for Bailey's induction into the Country Music Hall of Fame. "If his name is ever on the ballot," Acuff said, "he'll have one vote from Roy Acuff."

In 2005, Bailey was, in fact, inducted into the hall of fame, the redemption of a musical legacy that David Morton had worked for more than thirty years to preserve. Morton first met Bailey in 1973, and the two of them became close friends. Morton was impressed by DeFord's story—how this diminutive African American man, afflicted by polio as a child, had negotiated the terrain of Jim Crow to make music that crossed racial barriers. As Bailey later put it, "The Black and the white all wanted to hear the same tune."

For more than fifteen years, Bailey was a legend. But then in 1941, he was abruptly fired from the Grand Ole Opry, caught in the curious crossfire of a corporate battle to license new songs. He was a stylist more than a composer, taking old tunes he learned as a boy, or those he liked by other artists, and creating renditions distinctively his own. He didn't understand the sudden demand that he write new songs, which could then be licensed by BMI, a new enterprise supported by the Opry.

George Hay, adding an ugly dimension to the story, described the firing this way: "Like some members of his race and others, DeFord was lazy. He knew about a dozen numbers, which he put on the air and recorded for a major company, but he refused to learn any more, even though the reward was great. He was our mascot and is still loved by the entire company."

For Bailey, the words cut deep. The personal insult and racial condescension were compounded by the fact that he had regarded Hay as a friend. He didn't talk about it much. He simply picked up his life and moved on. He played his harmonica every day—it was his only addiction, he said—but he seldom performed in public any more. Instead, he made his living shining shoes.

"I knowed I could make it on my own," he told David Morton.

But, as Morton discovered, Bailey worried about how he might be remembered, fearful that history would misunderstand him.

"I promised him," Morton said in an interview, "that I would mark his grave and tell his story."

A definitive, well-crafted biography, first published in 1991, now rereleased with new material, was a major step in keeping that promise. As a collaborator, Morton turned to Charles Wolfe, a widely published English professor at Middle Tennessee State University, who had written extensively about country music.

But there was more to Morton's commitment. In the latter years of Bailey's life, he also arranged for strategic interviews (including one I did for *Country Music* magazine) and occasional performances that he thought would raise his friend's profile.

Under Morton's prodding, Bailey made several appearances on the Opry, both at the Ryman Auditorium and the newer facility at Opryland. He also performed on Night Train, a radio show on Nashville's WLAC aimed primarily at a Black audience, and was featured posthumously in Ken Burns's PBS series "Country Music."

Bailey's legacy has continued to grow. In 2022, Old Crow Medicine Show debuted a new song titled "DeFord Bailey Rides Again." And in 2023, Ketch Secor, the band's lead singer, persuaded the Opry to apologize formally for Bailey's firing.

For David Morton, there is now a symmetry to the story—"it's incredibly satisfying," he told me—and he and Wolfe end their book with Bailey's own words:

I want you to tell the world about this Black man. He ain't no fool. Just let people know what I am . . . I take the bitter with the sweet. Every day is Sunday with me. I'm happy-go-lucky.

"Amen!"

The Chancellor

Any list of the greatest educators of the twentieth century—Booker T. Washington, Benjamin Mays, Frank Porter Graham—would almost certainly include Chancellor Alexander Heard, who led Vanderbilt University during the tumultuous years from 1963 to 1972. During that time, when students at Berkeley and other universities demonstrated in pursuit of free speech, which was being denied them, Heard was a resolute supporter of the open forum and the right of students to speak their minds. Having been a student at Vanderbilt during that time, I was asked by *Vanderbilt Magazine* to reflect on the chancellor's legacy on the occasion of his death. Writing this column, which was one of several articles the magazine published about Heard, was a singular honor in my work as a writer.

It happened again and again in the 1960s. Chancellor Alexander Heard would appear at a Vanderbilt basketball game—one of his favorite pastimes back in those days—and as he made his way to his courtside seat, the entire student body would stand to applaud. All across the nation these were days of student unrest, and more and more as the decade progressed, there were activist stirrings at Vanderbilt as well. But the rebellion was never directed at Heard.

On the contrary, most of us in school at that time, especially those who knew him well, regarded the chancellor with a respect that shaded almost into awe. Part of it was simply his accessibility. Once at a "meeting of the university," events that were usually held in the spring at which students could ask anything they chose, a young woman rose to question the dress code. Was it really true, she demanded to know, that women students were forbidden to wear shorts on campus except to play tennis? And were they expected to wear raincoats on their way to the courts?

The dean of women, one of maybe twenty administrators arrayed on the stage to answer such questions, replied a little officiously that those indeed were the expectations. "Well," said the student, growing testy herself, "how about a plastic, see-through raincoat?"

There was a moment of tension that Heard broke with a smile. "There goes the dress code," he said, and with that, the issue seemed to be settled.

The chancellor was never a stickler for rules, at least not the silly and artificial ones. He believed that students, in large measure, should govern themselves, for how else could they make their way in the world? As historian Paul Conkin would later conclude, Heard saw Vanderbilt as "a place where pleas for fuller freedom could be calmly heard."

The most demanding test of that philosophy came in the spring of 1967, when the student-run Impact Symposium invited, among others, Black power advocate Stokely Carmichael to appear on campus. Only a few years earlier, such an invitation might have been unremarkable. Carmichael had worked as a Student Nonviolent Coordinating Committee organizer in some of the toughest places in the South, winning the respect of local Black leaders for what one of them called his "hip and fear-no-evil style." They knew that he carried a .22 pistol, but they also knew he didn't want to use it, preferring instead to rely on his wits.

By 1967, however, Carmichael had become, theoretically at least, an advocate of violence in pursuit of Black freedom. At Vanderbilt he delivered a well-reasoned address, introducing many of us to the concept of institutionalized racism—the notion that injustice in the country went deeper than the bigotry of sick individuals. But he also spoke the same day on the African American side of town, shouting Black power slogans that were followed by a riot. Some in Nashville blamed Vanderbilt, and specifically the chancellor, for refusing to rein in the unruly students who were responsible for Carmichael's visit to the city.

"Nothing that could be said in the way of apology," declared the *Nashville Banner*, "can remove the stench of Stokely Carmichael's visit." At a Vanderbilt Board of Trust meeting on May 5, 1967, there were some who wanted Heard to "eat crow," as one historian would later put it. The chancellor responded with an unflinching calm. He rejected the offers of some of his allies to push through a vote of confidence by the board, contending instead that the Carmichael visit was simply routine, requiring no action by the trustees.

It was, Heard explained, a case of the university "being a university."

"It hardly seems necessary," he said, "to burden you with a defense of the free exchange of ideas, or of the freedom to hear and the freedom to read for our students, or of the educational value of these freedoms."

In the weeks that followed that persuasive talk, Heard won national acclaim for his stand—and for Vanderbilt. For many of us who were students, meanwhile, he made an impression that never went away. In all of our meetings regarding Impact, there was never a moment—and I mean, not one—where he displayed the faintest trace of cynicism or departed from the public principles he espoused. To me, among many others, he put a human face on the definition of integrity.

Of all the things I learned at Vanderbilt, nothing was more important than that.

Madness
The Agony and Triumph of Elyn Saks

This profile of a remarkable woman was written for *Vanderbilt Magazine*.

Elyn Saks feels right at home on the University of Southern California campus. There is something about the leafy-green trees and ivy-covered walls, the slate-roofed buildings, and the perpetual warmth of the California climate that has put her at ease almost from the start. But even here in this academic cloister, where her office is cluttered with her legal research, where she holds an endowed professorship of law, and where she has earned the admiration of her peers, the same old voices keep drifting in. She hears them two or three times a day, bearing messages that she would rather keep at bay.

You are bad. You are evil. You have killed thousands of people with your thoughts.

She has been receiving these messages for much of her life, certainly since her days at Vanderbilt, where she graduated first in her class but sometimes alarmed her friends and fellow students with behavior that seemed far more than peculiar. She didn't yet know, when she was still an undergraduate, that she was falling into the grip of schizophrenia, and that her "journey through madness," as she would later put it, would be unbearably painful and long.

There was the night at Vanderbilt, for example, a frigid winter evening when the ground outside was covered with snow. Saks was talking with a visitor in her dorm, when suddenly and without any warning, she grabbed a blanket and rushed outside. She ran manically across the lawn, spreading her arms and pretending to fly.

"No one can get me!" she shouted in a frenzy. "I'm flying! I've escaped!"

Later she said it was all just a joke, just a moment of silliness that had swept her away. But the episodes grew worse over time, particularly after she left Vanderbilt in 1977 and entered the master's program at Oxford University. She had won a Marshall Scholarship to study in England, but something was unsettling about the move, and soon she found that she was losing her grip. She began handing in papers that were masses of gibberish, and muttering to herself as she walked through the town: *I am a bad person; I deserve to suffer. People are talking about me. Look at them; they're staring at me.*

She soon wound up in a mental hospital, and many years later she wrote down her memories of those times: "In my fog of isolation and silence, I began to feel I was receiving commands to do things—such as walk all by myself through the old abandoned tunnels that lay underneath the hospital. The origin of the commands was unclear. In my mind, they were issued by some sort of beings. Not real people with names or faces, but shapeless, powerful beings that controlled me with my thoughts. . . . *Walk through the tunnels and repent. Now lie down and don't move. You must be still. You are evil.*"

All of that was nearly thirty years ago, and in the time since then Saks has pulled herself from the cold and terrifying depths of her illness to build a distinguished career as a scholar. She is happily married and surrounded by friends, and a visitor to her office at the University of Southern California will encounter little evidence of the agony she's endured. But she recently decided to write it all down, to create a memoir of her own psychosis, believing that it might give hope to other people. Her powerful book *The Center Cannot Hold* was published by Hyperion in the summer of 2007, and within a few weeks the praise was pouring in.

Publishers Weekly called the book "engrossing." The *Washington Post* praised Saks's "lucidity and intelligence." *Time* magazine selected her story as one of the ten best books of 2007. But at least as important in Saks's own mind was the warm response of her colleagues and friends. She had felt she was skating where the ice was thin, where the people she knew might easily be repelled, and where the university that had nurtured her career might find her revelations embarrassing. But none of that happened. Instead, people praised her honesty and courage, and marveled at the simple power of her story. And her memoir does have a strength all its own—a journey of suffering and a road to recovery that will probably never quite come to an end; a passage through a schizophrenic nightmare that is far more common than many people know.

But hers, in the end, is a story of hope—of "a brilliant mind," as *Time* magazine put it, that with love and therapy and the right kind of medicine finally, painfully learned to heal itself. There was a time, however, when it was hard to believe that such a triumph could occur.

The worst of it came when she entered law school.

After four years of study, she had received her master's degree from Oxford and decided to take on the challenges of Yale. Her illness, at best, was still unresolved. She had already spent months in a mental hospital, and then in intensive psychoanalysis. But in between her bouts of psychosis, she managed to do well enough in her studies to be accepted at the law school of her choice, which turned out to be Yale. She arrived in New Haven accustomed to academic success, but knowing also that changes in her life often triggered major problems—a powerful feeling of dislocation that would degenerate into a break with reality.

Sure enough, within two weeks of her arrival at Yale, as she walked among the great gothic buildings with their stained-glass windows and drafty hallways, she began having thoughts that were not her own, and began seeing people who were not really there. One of them was a bearded man with a knife who was ready to kill her. On an autumn weekend in 1982, with her symptoms getting worse, she made her way to the student health center, babbling wildly to anyone who would listen. *There's the killing fields. Heads exploding. I didn't do anything wrong. They just said "quake, fake, lake." I used to ski. Are you trying to kill me?* The doctors tried to reassure her, but she pulled away and crawled under a desk, moaning softly as she rocked back and forth. *They're killing me. They're killing me. I've got to try. Die. Lie. Cry.*

They sent her off to another mental hospital, where she lay for thirty hours on one of the beds, her arms and legs bound by restraints and a net tied over the rest of her body. She found that she couldn't move at all, and no matter how desperately she begged for relief—"Please," she cried, "it's not necessary"—the doctors assured her that this was really best.

A quarter century later she remembers that medieval moment as clearly as if it had just happened to her, and her anger still ripples through the pages of her memoir: "As frightened as I was, I was equally angry, and frantic to find a way to show defiance—not an easy task when you're in four-point restraints and pinned under a tuna net. I was bound . . . but not gagged! So I inhaled as deeply as I could, and started belting out some beloved Beethoven. Not, for obvious reasons, *Ode to Joy*, but Beethoven's Fifth Symphony. BA-BA BA! BA-BA-BA BA! Look, there, see how he created such power out of those four simple notes! It echoed nicely down the halls, so I did it again."

Her brother, Warren Saks, came to visit her a few days later, and he was stunned to see how awful she looked—gaunt and wild eyed with her hair all askew, and so thin it was startling. She had always been tall, nearly five foot ten, and sometimes underweight, but nothing prepared him for the pain in her face. "It was frightening," he remembered. "It was really clear how sick she was."

For a younger brother who had always loved and admired his sister, who was astonished by her brilliance and moved by the warmth she showed to other people, it was nearly too painful to see her this way. And yet even then, he couldn't really grasp the depths of her agony or the fundamental gloom of her official prognosis: "Grave," one doctor wrote at the time. "Chronic paranoid schizophrenia with acute exacerbation."

For much of the medical community in the 1980s, such a diagnosis was like a death sentence or, more precisely, the prediction of a life without any hope. Her condition was one that didn't have a cure, a chemical malfunction afflicting her brain that would sever her ties to the rational world, in a sense to the world of physical reality, where most of the human population lived. She might well spend her life under lock and key, and whenever her symptoms spiraled out of control—when she began to talk about killing or tried to run away—there would be no choice but to tie her down, fill her full of drugs, and wait for the terrible moment to pass.

Such was the view of her doctors at Yale.

The fact that Saks has defied those predictions is a testament in part to her stubbornness and will. But it was a facet of her character often played out in double-edged ways—in a refusal at first to believe she was sick, which sometimes made her resistant to treatment, even as it kept her from ever giving up. She was determined, for example, during her slides into madness, not to let go of her academic work, her studies of philosophy and the law, and later her teaching, writing, and research. She had grown up in Miami in a strong Jewish family, among people who managed to build meaningful lives, and it seldom occurred to her not to do the same.

It was true periodically that the agony of her illness would sweep her away, that the voices and thoughts taking hold of her mind would become so powerful and so terrifying that she was reduced to desperation and despair. But when the antipsychotic drugs did their job, turning down the volume to give her some relief, she would find a part of herself still intact—still determined to find fulfillment in her work, and still tied to her family and her circle of friends.

And yet, for Saks, the issue of her medication was a problem. It was clear to her doctors that she simply had to have it, for that was the nature of schizophrenia itself: a chemical imbalance affecting her brain. But Saks saw pharmacology as a crutch—a view that may have been a throwback to the antidrug messages she had listened to in high school. In those days of chemical experimentation, when she and her peers were getting into trouble, Elyn accepted the mantra of drug counselors that a person had to have the strength to stay clean. It was a matter of will more than anything else. And later in her life, when schizophrenic notions invaded her brain, her greatest fear was not that she was ill but that she didn't have the strength to repel them.

"I truly believed," she would write in her memoir, "that everyone had the same scrambled thoughts that I did, as well as the occasional breaks from reality and the sense that some unseen force was compelling them to destructive behavior. The difference was, others were simply more adept than I at masking the craziness and presenting a healthy, competent front to the world."

And others, of course, managed to do it without the help of medication.

Eventually, however, after years of suffering, her resistance wore down. Again and again, whatever her doctors' choice of drugs, she would try to wean herself from their prescriptions. And again and again she would fall apart. But finally, in California, she was introduced to clozapine, a drug developed in part through the studies of Dr. Herbert Meltzer of Vanderbilt, and it has worked well for her—for the most part, keeping her psychotic symptoms at bay.

Through it all, she also has relied on psychoanalysis, which she says is not typical of schizophrenic patients. Many psychiatrists, Saks explains, believe her form of mental illness is basically "a random firing of neurons," producing jumbled thoughts that are beyond the reach of any kind of rationality. And indeed, when Saks began seeing an analyst in Oxford, the first few sessions were downright scary. As she remembered it later, despite the fact that she had never been violent, she carried a box cutter inside her purse, as well as a kitchen knife with a serrated blade, and warned the analyst that she had better watch her step.

"You are an evil monster," Saks hissed, "perhaps the devil. I won't let you kill me. You are evil, a witch. I'll fight."

But the analyst was calm, and session after session, day after day, she pushed Saks to confront her most frightening thoughts. For Saks the effect was strangely reassuring, a gradual discovery that she had found a safe place to deal with her illness. Thoughts that she had simply tried to repress were now being dissected and robbed of their power—and her analyst, always firm and professional, never seemed to be repelled. Even today, with her life going well, she sees her analyst five mornings a week, sometimes sorting through psychotic thoughts, other times talking about ordinary things, the routine ups and downs of her life.

"I'm a lifer," she says of her therapy. "I'm just too scared to get out of it."

And so it appears that after a long and difficult journey—from Vanderbilt to Oxford and then to Yale, from a teaching job at a Connecticut law school, and finally to the University of Southern California—Saks has found the tools she needs to survive: a blend of medication and psychoanalysis. But there have been other ingredients in her healing also, things as ordinary as they were indispensable. One of those is a strong circle of friends, people such as Scott Altman, a law school colleague, who works in an office just down the hall.

Altman met Saks in 1989, just after her arrival at USC, and he found her fascinating from the start. She was tall and very bright, with a long, angular face that seemed to break easily into a smile. He says he had no inkling of her mental illness, though in retrospect there were a few things that might have made him wonder. Saks seemed extraordinarily shy, and delivered her lectures in class sitting down, as if she didn't want to call attention to herself. But she was brilliant in her course on mental health and the law, and in all her discussions with her students and peers, Altman was struck by what he later called "her careful, thoughtful intellectual contributions."

He knew that she worked exceptionally hard. Between 1989 and 2002, before she started writing her personal memoir, she published three scholarly books and contributed chapters to at least three more, all the while writing more than thirty different articles for legal, psychiatric, and medical journals. For all of that she was rewarded by the University of Southern California with a special appointment as Orrin B. Evans Professor of Law and Psychiatry and the Behavioral Sciences. But to her friends in California, the most impressive thing about Saks is something from a more everyday realm: her simple ability to be a friend.

"Elyn makes many friends," explains Altman, "and usually keeps track of them forever. She is very funny and laughs easily at other people's jokes. But in difficult times, when people around us go through deaths, divorce, or cancer, Elyn is almost always the most aggressive about reaching out. She visits people in the hospital or whatever, and never shies away from those circumstances."

For all of those reasons, Altman and others took it in stride when they encountered one of Elyn's psychotic breaks. They were becoming less frequent by the time she arrived in Southern California, but then one day in 1999 she learned in the course of a routine physical that she had breast cancer. The irony of it was, the diagnosis came as she was getting engaged. She had met Will Vinet, a law librarian at the university and a man of optimism and talent, who wore his hair in a ponytail and loved to play music, cook gourmet dinners, and build fine furniture with his own hands. Elyn had made many friends through the years, but after meeting Will she realized she had never been in love. And now at the pinnacle of her own good fortune, she was suddenly confronted with the possibility of death. When she heard the diagnosis, something snapped inside her, and she began to babble once again in a free association of schizophrenic thoughts.

Fleeces and geeses and astronomical proportions with people growing tumors. It's a growth industry.

As it happened, a friend was in the doctor's waiting room, a Los Angeles psychiatrist named Esther Fine. She took Elyn into her arms and told her gently, "Oh, honey, it's going to be all right. You're in good hands."

The psychosis passed more quickly this time, and after the surgery and radiation, the cancer also has remained in remission. Elyn married Will, who remains a stabilizing force in her life, which is, she says, richer and better than it ever has been. But she also knows, probably better than most, that things can always blow at any seam.

It is a December morning in Southern California, and Saks is working alone in her office. As always, there are the stray and random schizophrenic thoughts—*You are evil. You have killed many people*—but she has learned over time to take them in stride, to treat them merely as the symptoms of an illness, no longer as crippling as they were in the past. She is focused instead on her legal and psychiatric scholarship, surrounded everywhere by mountains of paper. She has embarked on a study of high-functioning people with schizophrenia, searching empirically for the keys to their success, and she wants to study ways to help mentally ill people seek treatment.

There are also issues of mental health and the law—the use of physical restraints in hospitals, the right of patients to refuse medication—and all of these studies add a feeling of structure and purpose to her life. Most weeks, in fact, she works every day, chipping away at her projects, but taking frequent breaks to call her friends on the phone. She talks every day to Stephen Behnke, with whom she wrote her first book, and to her LA friends such as Janet Smith and Esther Fine. And of course there is Will.

"My true love," she calls him. "He gives my life a meaning that I never thought possible."

But there is also the haunting reality of her illness, a reality, she knows, that will never go away. "I feel sad," she admits. "So many years of so much pain." And yet she believes her story offers hope, and she is now happy to have shared it with other people. There is a sturdy consolation in that—for her, another source of meaning and strength, still another reason to keep pushing on.

Epilogue, 2023

As this book goes to press, Elyn Saks still serves as Orrin B. Evans Professor of Law at the University of Southern California, and as faculty director of the Saks Institute for Mental Health Law, Policy, and Ethics, which she founded after receiving a $500,000 "genius grant" from the MacArthur Foundation.

Helen Keller
Monument to a Radical Idealist

During the raging national debate over Confederate iconography, I wrote this article for *Alabama Heritage*, describing a moment when my state got it right—more right, actually, than its officials may have realized.

There is a photo making the rounds on the Internet—an image of children at the U.S. Capitol, gazing into the face of Helen Keller, touching the Braille inscription at the base of her statue. Since 2009, the bronze likeness of Keller has represented Alabama in Statuary Hall, a gift from the state legislature, made at the urging of Governor Bob Riley and his wife, Patsy.

Keller is seven years old in this sculpture, created by South Dakota artist Edward Hlavka. It is a work of extraordinary beauty, depicting a mythic event that Keller says "awakened my soul" to the richness and possibilities of life. Clearly it has the same effect on children. They come to this place, more hallowed than most in the halls of Congress, and many of them know already the story behind this frozen moment now larger than life. Helen is a little girl in Tuscumbia, Alabama, deaf, blind, and unable to speak, rendered that way by a fever that came when she was not yet two. But she has a teacher, a "miracle worker" named Anne Sullivan, who has led her to the water pump. As the liquid falls gently onto Helen's hand, Sullivan, with her finger, spells out the word, "W-A-T-E-R" on her pupil's palm.

The children at the statue know a little of the story after that—how Keller soon learned to read and speak, and overcame the most cruel and impossible of odds. As Governor Riley declared at the statue's dedication, "Courage and strength can exist in the most unlikely places. Children especially need to be reminded of this."

But it may simply be in the nature of monuments that they oversimplify as much as they reveal. Keller's predecessor in Statuary Hall might have become a lightning rod for controversy if the sculpture had not been replaced when it was. Jabez Curry had been a Confederate officer, a proponent of slavery and secession, and thus precisely the kind of figure whose image might have angered the critics of Confederate iconography. There was, in fact, more to Curry's life. After the war, he became one of the leading educators of his time—a tireless advocate of public education who was also the founding president for what is now Samford University.

He traveled the South, once covering seventeen thousand miles in a single year, promoting public schools for all children, including African Americans, as well as industrial education for Blacks and poor whites. Education was, he thought, not only the key to progress but also a way to heal old wounds and release the full power of human potential, regardless of race. In the gathering public debate over monuments, would Curry's legacy have been oversimplified or dismissed? Would his advocacy of slavery have been disqualifying—a tainted reminder of the Lost Cause, unworthy of being honored in a public space?

We may never know, for Curry's statue was moved to Samford University and replaced at the Capitol by the sculpture of Keller. She seemed a safe and inspirational choice. But here again, the story is more complicated than many visitors to Statuary Hall might suppose. As Alabama poet Jeanie Thompson notes, Keller was not a perpetual child but a woman who emerged as a writer in twentieth century, and championed some of the most controversial causes of her time.

"Helen Keller was one of the most radically engaged individuals to walk this earth," says Thompson, author of *The Myth of Water: Poems from the Life of Helen Keller*. "Her deafblind condition only increased her boundless empathy."

In one of her earliest public lectures, delivered in 1913, Keller began a sweeping critique of social conditions in America—and in much of the world beyond. "I do not like this world as it is," she declared, and added in a magazine article, "I must face unflinchingly a world of facts—a world of misery, degradation, blindness, sin, a world struggling against the elements, against the unknown, against itself. How to reconcile this world of fact with the bright world of my own imagining? My darkness had been filled with the light of intelligence, and behold the outer day-lit world was stumbling and groping in social blindness."

"For a time I was depressed," she told the *New York Times*, "but little by little my confidence came back and I realized that the wonder is not that conditions are so bad, but that humanity has advanced so far in spite of them. I am now in the fight to change things."

One of her earliest concerns was the issue of race. Born in 1880, Keller was herself the daughter of a prominent newspaper editor who had once owned slaves. She felt the issue in a personal way: "Ashamed in my very soul, I behold in my beloved southland the tears of those who are oppressed," she wrote in a letter endorsing the work of the NAACP. She became a supporter of that organization, newly founded in 1909 in response to violence against African Americans, and contributed to its magazine, *The Crisis*. In a letter to a friend, she wrote, "The continued lynchings and other crimes against Negroes, whether in New England or the South, and the unspeakable political exponents of white supremacy, according to all recorded history, augur ill for America's future."

Keller also supported the women's movement, which, in the early years of the twentieth century, had two primary—and sometimes separate—objectives. One of those was the right to vote, a suffragist crusade culminating in 1920 with the ratification of the Nineteenth Amendment. The other was access to "birth control," a phrase coined by Margaret Sanger, who believed from her experience as a nurse, when she saw women die from too many pregnancies, that every woman must be "the absolute mistress of her own body." In the early twentieth century, as Sanger began her advocacy of that goal, any mention of contraception was illegal—a violation of an antiobscenity statute called the Comstock Law. Sanger was indicted under that law and fled to Europe to avoid prosecution. There, she discovered diaphragms and, once again risking prosecution, began an effort to smuggle them into the United States.

Helen Keller embraced her as a friend. She also supported the suffragist movement, declaring pointedly in a speech in Chicago, "The inferiority of women is man-made."

But it was in the realm of economics that Keller was at her most controversial. She became a member of the Socialist Party, citing as her inspiration not only the writings of Karl Marx but also the words of Jesus Christ. "Truly, He has said," she declared in an interview with the *New York Tribune*, "'Woe unto you that will permit the least of mine to suffer.'" It was not, however, such statements of principle that most infuriated Keller's critics, or eventually landed her on an FBI watch list. More specifically, she backed labor strikes by textile workers, copper miners, and others she regarded as deliberate victims of "the capitalist class." By 1912 she cast her lot with the most radical wing of the labor movement, the International Workers of the World.

Eight years later, Keller became a founding member of the American Civil Liberties Union, an organization committed to constitutional rights, even for champions of unpopular causes. For all of this, she paid a price. In 1914, the editors of the *Detroit Free Press* delivered a rebuke, as patronizing as it was common among those who did not share her politics: "Helen Keller, struggling to point the way to the light for the deaf, dumb and blind is inspiring. Helen Keller preaching socialism; Helen Keller passing on the merits of the copper strike; Helen Keller under these aspects is pitiful."

Keller's response was defiant, rooted in the certainty that she was right. "I feel like Joan of Arc at times," she said. "My whole being becomes uplifted."

There came a time, however, when disillusionment set in—a profound realization that she lived in a country that was slow to change. In the 1930s, as the world careened toward war, she railed against the failure of the United States to take in more refugees from Hitler's genocide—including, especially, people with disabilities. When the war was over, Keller traveled to Japan and visited Hiroshima and Nagasaki. She touched the twisted buildings and trees, the scarred face of a survivor, and all of it, she said, "scorched a deep scar" on her own soul. She grieved as well about Black soldiers who had fought for freedom and returned to a country that still denied it to people of color.

By the 1950s, burdened by such disappointments, she confided to friends that she was beginning to feel "old" and "tired." In 1961, at the age of eighty, she made her last public speech, supporting greater educational opportunities for "children who are physically, mentally, or emotionally handicapped." She was still determined, she said, despite the sobering developments of the twentieth century, to raise her voice as an advocate and writer—a woman with visibility and presence, trying do what she could to make things better.

Helen Keller died in 1968, just a few weeks short of her eighty-eighth birthday. She left a legacy that began in an inspirational moment, depicted now at the U.S. Capitol, and grew steadily larger over the course of her life.

"To help others," concluded Jeanie Thompson, "she opened her heart to the world. Her example should catapult us into action today."

Little School on a Hill

This essay, adapted from a children's book, *Ezra Wants to Know: The True Story of the Rosenwald Schools,* which I coauthored with educator Marti Rosner, was published in *Alabama Heritage.*

On a fall day in 1911, Julius Rosenwald, president of Sears, Roebuck and Company, boarded a train headed south from Chicago, Illinois. He was traveling with Emil Hirsch, his rabbi at the Chicago Sinai Congregation, who had emerged by the early twentieth century as a powerful spokesman for social justice in America. The two men shared a passionate concern for the oppression of African Americans, having observed, among other things, the similarities between the anti-Jewish pogroms that swept the Russian empire between 1881 and 1884 and the wave of anti-Black violence at the end of Reconstruction in the United States. Ugliness and terror reigned in the south of both countries.

The men were on their way to Alabama to meet with Booker T. Washington, founder and president of Tuskegee Institute. Rosenwald was already a donor to African American causes, including the newly founded National Association for the Advancement of Colored People, where leaders such as W. E. B. Du Bois gave voice to a more militant view of Black progress than the one supported by Washington. For his part, Rosenwald—who had presided over a time of unprecedented prosperity at Sears, Roebuck and Company—was eager to find a channel through which his philanthropy could do the most good.

At Tuskegee he could see with a sudden and tangible clarity what Washington had in mind for his people. Here was a handsome campus spread across gently rolling hills, its buildings designed by Robert Taylor, the first African American architect to graduate from M.I.T., constructed with bricks handmade by students who attended the school. In Washington's mind, there was nothing more important than education, and as he and Rosenwald talked about such things, the great educator lamented the scarcity of schools for Black children in the rural South. They agreed to work on the problem together, and the result of that meeting of the minds was one of the great undertakings in American philanthropy—the construction by the early 1930s of nearly five thousand schools across fifteen southern and border states.

They began their ambitious project in the area around Tuskegee. There are scattered memorials to that effort—a historical marker in the village of Loachapoaka, where the first school was built—and on a lonely hillside between Tuskegee and the town of Notasulga, one of the early schools still stands. It is a museum and community center today, having been restored by a group of citizens led by some of its former students.

The Shiloh Rosenwald School, named for the Shiloh Missionary Baptist Church that provided the land, was one of the six original schools built in 1913, as Washington and Rosenwald proceeded cautiously with their plans. After the original building mysteriously burned, a fate not uncommon for Rosenwald schools, as white supremacists across the South attacked the symbols of African American progress, the current structure was rebuilt in 1922. For the next four decades, says former student Barbara Moseley, "this school was a hall of learning."

With the coming of desegregation, the two-room school finally closed its doors in 1964. By the early years of the new millennium, the building was in need of major renovations.

In 2006, Elizabeth "Liz" Ware Sims, an administrator at Auburn University, who was also a Shiloh alumnus, founded the Shiloh Community Restoration Foundation to try to save the historic structure. The foundation, mostly led by Shiloh alumni, began with a $50,000 grant administered by the National Trust for Historic Preservation and worked with architecture students at Auburn and nearby Tuskegee University, where the Rosenwald school idea was born.

In 2010 the school and church were added to the National Register of Historic Places, and visitors were soon making their way to the newly refurbished Shiloh-Rosenwald School. Some were content to read the historical marker out front or peer through the windows of the building. But others made appointments to tour the site and hear stories from the foundation members about Shiloh's beginnings.

From the start, Rosenwald required local communities to match seed money provided by the philanthropist, thus assuring that the schools were a source of pride, not merely an act of charity. According to research by the Society of Architectural Historians, Black citizens living near Shiloh more than matched the Rosenwald grant of $800.

"These were proud people," said Felicia Chandler, current chair of the foundation. "They were not sharecroppers, but independent farmers who owned their land. They saw a chance for something better."

On a visit by the authors of this article, Chandler and other board members recalled their time as students at the school. Yes, they said, there were only two classrooms, one serving grades one through three, the other grades four through six. In the early years, there was no electricity in this part of Alabama, so on cold winter mornings, the rooms were heated only by the sun streaming through the nearly floor-to-ceiling east-facing windows, and potbellied stoves. It fell to the boys in the upper grades to gather wood to start the fires and to the girls to sweep the floors and keep the building clean. The two outhouses (one for girls, the other for boys) stood near the trees far behind the school. Books and desks were often handed down from white schools.

But for Shiloh alumni, their memories of the school are not a story of deprivation. During their morning routine, along with the Pledge of Allegiance, they recited a slogan taught to them by their first-grade teacher: "Good, better, best ... never let it rest, until the good is better and the better is best." They remember the demands of dedicated teachers, as well as plays and pageants and musical programs supported by an active PTA, performed for members of the community. They speak with pride of the accomplishments of former Shiloh students such as Barbara Mahone, a General Motors executive appointed by President Reagan in 1982 as chair of the Federal Labor Relations Authority.

"There's a myth about Black education being inferior," said Dr. Paulette Dilworth, vice president for Diversity, Equity, and Inclusion at the University of Alabama–Birmingham, speaking at Shiloh's Annual Legacy Gala in April 2018. "We can dispel that myth."

All of this is a part of the story preserved and celebrated at the Shiloh Rosenwald School. But there is another, darker chapter as well. On the same piece of ground, an ancient oak tree stands between the schoolhouse and the Shiloh Missionary Baptist Church. It was on a bench at the foot of that oak that participants became unknowing victims recruited for the infamous Tuskegee Syphilis Study.

Starting in 1932, six hundred African American men, 399 of whom had latent syphilis, agreed to participate in a study conducted by doctors from the U.S. Public Health Service. They were told they were being treated for "bad blood," but they were given no effective treatment at all, even after penicillin became widely available in 1947. The study ended in 1972, but it was not until May 16, 1997, that President Clinton, speaking on behalf of the U.S. government, apologized for the crime. "What the United States government did was shameful," he said, "and I am sorry."

All of this is remembered at the same historical site: a Baptist church founded in 1870 as an assertion of African American independence; a "School of Hope," one of the original six built during a shining moment in American philanthropy; and the Shiloh Cemetery just down the hill, where more participants in the Syphilis Study are buried than at any other site.

"This place," concluded Shiloh alumna Barbara Mahone, "truly represents the best of mankind and the worst of mankind." But in the end, she said, there was one unassailable fact: "People like me were the beneficiaries of an education second to none."

Reflecting on the larger legacy of Rosenwald Schools, which began at Shiloh and the area around it, activist-historian Julian Bond put it this way: "It's a wonderful story of cooperation between this philanthropist who did not have to care about Black people, but who did, and who expended his considerable wealth in ensuring that they got their fair shake in America." He called it a high point in the philanthropy of justice—in the early years of the twentieth century, a "path-breaking" moment in the history of the South.

The Odyssey of Chief Calvin McGhee

> This is the story of an Indian chief of the mid-twentieth century who led his people from the depths of poverty to a renaissance of identity and pride. I wrote it for *Alabama Heritage*.

At the turning of the new millennium, many of the elders were still amazed by the way things had changed. Ruthie Mae Rackard was one of those. As a member of the Poarch Band of Creek Indians, she remembered the days when the greatest Indian confederacy in the South was reduced to a hovel of rundown houses. The people lived hard and close to the land—in communities like Poarch and Head of Perdido, where families of two or three generations crowded together in rough-hewn cabins and braced themselves against the heat or the cold or the vagaries of poverty and racial segregation. They worked as farmers, loggers, sharecroppers, migrants—whatever they could find to do with their hands—and those who dreamed of a better life would sometimes stand and stare in dismay as the school buses passed their children on the road.

In 1948, a farmer by the name of Calvin McGhee, Ruthie Mae Rackard's older brother, finally got tired of the problem with the buses. McGhee was chief of the Poarch Creek Band. He was one of the most successful members of the community, raising his hogs and cattle, peanuts and corn—a man of ambition who wanted to see better things for his children. His sister remembered his fury—or at least his air of pointed resolve—when it came to the school bus. He thought it should stop for Indian children, and he made that case to officials in the county. "He just told 'em," Rackard recalled, "'You're gonna stop, or I'm gonna know why.'"

All across the South, as it happened, buses had become a symbol of oppression. That same year, in Clarendon County, South Carolina, a group of African Americans went to school officials in this remote outback of cotton fields and blackwater swamps, and demanded a school bus for their children. These were men who came home from World War II, shocked anew by the realities of prejudice, the denial of the freedoms for which they had fought. Like the Indians in Alabama, they could see no reason why school buses stopped for white children only. But a county official told them bluntly, "We ain't got no money to provide a bus for your n——- children." Stung by this obscene rebuff, the parents called Thurgood Marshall, the country's most prominent civil rights lawyer, and soon they escalated their demands from a bus to the total dismantling of segregated schools.

The Clarendon case became one of five that led to the landmark U.S. Supreme Court ruling of 1954 that declared segregated schools unconstitutional. The following year in Montgomery, African Americans boycotted city buses to demand an end to segregation laws that relegated Blacks to the back of the bus. Once again, the Supreme Court ruled in their favor, and buses, a perennial reminder of oppression, also became a symbol of change.

This was true for the Poarch Creeks as well. Not only was the school bus issue the culminating moment in a twenty-year struggle for better education, the events that followed would thrust Calvin McGhee into a leadership role among Native Americans, and in vast and still unexpected ways, would transform the lives of the Indian people in Escambia County, Alabama. Seminal victories came in 1949 in the form of a school bus and a new public school for Indian children, though they still faced the inequity of segregated schools. In her 2007 Harvard University dissertation "The Muskogee Education Movement" and in other writings, Dr. Deidra Dees, tribal archivist and director of Poarch Creek Archives and Records Management, interviewed tribal elders who remembered that movement and its connection to the larger history of the tribe.

One of them, Roberta McGhee Sells, recounted stories handed down in her family since the Trail of Tears in the 1830s. "The old people," she told Dr. Dees, "told us about Andrew Jackson driving people out like cows. And that's what made Indian people so afraid of white folks. To hear and know how they was treated . . . I can understand why they was afraid."

Sells's great-great-grandmother and -grandfather, Semoice and Lynn McGhee, managed to escape removal through a complicated quirk of history. In a sense, their story began on a hot August day in 1813 when a band of Creeks attacked Fort Mims, a flimsy stockade in southern Alabama, killing nearly all of the settlers inside. Some of the dead were white; others were mixed-race Creeks, caught in what became a civil war, as the Muscogee people—the name they used before the white people came—split over how to respond to the growing encroachment on their land. Many of the more traditional Muscogees were inspired by the vision of Tecumseh, a Shawnee chief from what is now Ohio, who came south in 1811 seeking to build a coalition of tribes capable of driving the white man to the sea. Tecumseh, who had familial ties to the Creeks, cut a terrifying figure when he met with their chiefs. His face was daubed with black war paint, and his straight, dark hair was shaved at the temples. A pair of crane feathers hung from his crown.

Some Creeks thought Tecumseh was a fool. There were too many whites for the Indians to fight, and at the council of chiefs in the Muscogee town of Tukabatchee, one of those who spoke for peace was Red Eagle, a mixed-blood warrior whose father was Scottish. To the whites he was known as William Weatherford, and he found himself caught between two worlds. Some of his neighbors wanted to retreat more deeply into Indian ways, and to take up arms if necessary to protect their traditional way of life. Others thought it was essential to adapt. As skirmishing began on the Alabama frontier, Red Eagle reluctantly cast his lot with the Red Sticks, as the traditionalist fighters came to be known. On August 30, 1813, he led the assault against Fort Mims. In a surprise attack in the middle of the day, Red Stick warriors rushed through the open gates of the fort and began to slaughter the people inside, refusing even to spare women and children. Red Eagle had warned against such carnage. He was not surprised by the retribution that followed.

In Tennessee, the legislature commissioned Andrew Jackson to go and "exterminate the Creek nation." Jackson did his best to oblige. With troops from Mississippi and Georgia, as well as Tennessee, plus a contingent of Cherokees, Choctaws, and Creeks (some of whom had lost family members at Fort Mims), Jackson embarked on a mission of slaughter that ended with the Battle of Horseshoe Bend. On March 27, 1814, more than eight hundred of the roughly one thousand Red Stick fighters led by Chief Menawa were killed in the fighting. Jackson reported that the Tallapoosa River, where the battle occurred, turned that day to the color of blood.

In the treaty of Fort Jackson that followed, the Creeks ceded more than twenty million acres to the United States. Those loyal to Jackson were given small grants of land. But when Jackson, as president, signed the Indian Removal Act of 1830, his policies of ethnic cleansing were aimed at his former allies as well.

In her interview with Dr. Dees, Roberta McGhee Sells remembered the story of her own family's fury. "They weren't about to move!" she said. "They were staying where they was at. This was our land!" Her ancestor, Lynn McGhee, was among the Creeks receiving land under the Treaty of Fort Jackson. In their effort to escape the Trail of Tears, some of the ancestors took their case to the Alabama court system and won. Others simply hid in the woods, sometimes in elaborate caves they dug themselves. In the end, only a small group remained, many of them retreating as far from the white world as they could.

"At least we didn't lose it all," said one elder, a trace of bitterness still in her voice.

Chief McGhee understood that feeling. As a descendant of people who tried to make peace, he would later declare that his quest for justice for the Poarch Creek Band—from the pursuit of education for Indian children to fair compensation for stolen land—sometimes made him identify with Red Eagle and other leaders of the Red Stick resistance. That history, he said, was like an open wound. Once on a trip to Washington, D.C., he was with a lawyer who suggested they visit a statue of Andrew Jackson. McGhee refused.

"I don't want to be in hell nor heaven, neither one with that man," he said.

Over the years, starting sometime around 1950, McGhee made many trips to the nation's capital. For the rest of his life, until he died in 1970, he worked on Indian claims to the land. He knew his people had been cheated, as had the members of many other tribes, and under the Indian Claims Commission Act, passed by Congress in 1946, he pursued compensation for land that was lost. It was a tedious process. Calvin's wife, Joyce McGhee, remembered the multiple visits she made with her husband to the National Archives and the Library of Congress. "You had to ask for exactly what you wanted or you didn't get it," she told anthropologist J. Anthony Paredes.

Fortunately, said Joyce, Calvin had a winning way with people, rooted primarily in his seriousness of purpose. One staff member at the National Archives "just fell in love with him," she said. "He knew my husband was interested in his people." With the help of such sympathetic staff members, McGhee traced the lineage of as many tribal members as he could to the time of the Creek War and the Treaty of Fort Jackson. Beyond the pursuit of compensation, for McGhee the mission was also spiritual—an affirmation of identity and pride.

"He was an Indian," said Joyce.

It was about this time that Calvin began to wear war bonnets, made for him by Joyce, on some of his visits to the nation's capital, particularly if those visits involved official meetings with members of Congress. "Calvin and I," Joyce said, "we met with practically all the Congressmen in the Congress building." Some people questioned his use of headdresses, which resembled those from the western plains more than anything worn by the ancestor Creeks. But to Calvin, she said, "his feathers represent power."

In the 1960s, he wore a war bonnet to meet with President Kennedy. His sister, Ruthie Mae Rackard, later told the story of one of those early meetings. Chief McGhee was waiting at the White House, nervous, perhaps about how a Native American from rural Alabama, even if he was a leader of his people, might fare in such a high-powered environment. So he pulled out a pen and an old envelope and began to scribble on the back, repeating while he waited the most reassuring line from the twenty-third Psalm: "The Lord is my shepherd ..."

Such was the faith and the hope that sustained him.

Joyce McGhee remembered how she watched him age. He seemed so young in the early days, tanned from his time in the Alabama sun, and from the blood of indigenous people in his veins. His face was smooth, nearly wrinkle-free. Over the years, nearly all of that would change, as McGhee not only pursued the land claims for the Poarch Band but also became deeply involved in the broader struggle for Native American rights. With leaders of other tribes, he helped to draft "The Declaration of Indian Purpose: The Voice of the American Indian."

It was a manifesto of sorts, adopted on June 20, 1961, at a meeting of indigenous leaders in Chicago. McGhee and the others offered this proclamation:

> We believe in the inherent right of all people to retain spiritual and cultural values, and that the free exercise of these values is necessary to the normal development of any people. Indians exercised this inherent right to live their own lives for thousands of years before the white man

came and took their lands. It is a more complex world in which Indians live today, but the Indian people who first settled the New World and built the great civilizations which only now are being dug out of the past, long ago demonstrated that they could master complexity.

We believe in the future of a greater America, an America which we were the first to love ...

In the Poarch Creek archives, there is a photo of Chief McGhee, dressed in his headdress and full regalia, taken August 15, 1962, as he and other Native American leaders presented the manifesto to President Kennedy. But he knew his work was not yet done. For another eight years, until his death from a heart attack on his way to the funeral of another tribal member, he continued to push the Creek land claims, and the restoration of Muscogee identity and culture. Privately, Joyce had to worry about him. "He had aged awful," she remembered. And yet it was true that by 1970, his work was beginning to bear fruit.

Nationally, issues affecting Native Americans were moving toward the forefront of concern. Two important books, *Custer Died for Your Sins*, written by Vince Deloria Jr., a Standing Rock Lakota from North Dakota, and *Bury My Heart at Wounded Knee*, written by the enormously empathetic Dee Brown, who was white, helped raise the profile of an Indian movement that was becoming more active. Organizations like the National Congress of American Indians, the National Indian Youth Council, and the American Indian Movement were, each in its own way, pursuing goals of cultural preservation and justice for indigenous people that had long been shared by Calvin McGhee.

Closer to home, there was progress with the Indian Claims Commission, resulting, shortly after McGhee's death, in a tribal settlement to pay for lost land. Payments to individual Creeks were modest, but the psychological implications were huge, laying the foundation for future progress. Eddie Tullis, who became tribal chairman in 1978, immediately began to pursue federal recognition for the Poarch Creek Band— an official finding by the U.S. government that they were, in fact, an indigenous community that had functioned as a tribe since before the Creek War. Gale Thrower, tribal archivist at that time, painstakingly built that case with the help of anthropologist Anthony Parades, and in 1984 federal recognition became a reality.

Tullis and other tribal leaders, including Buford Rolin and Houston McGhee, knew that housing was a critical need. And with the federal money that was now available, they could build infrastructure as well—roads and sewers, a tribal headquarters, a new health clinic—plus 160 new houses. From there they could work on the economy and education, and soon it would be a different kind of place. No longer would the Indians have to leave to get a job, and those who had drifted away in the past would now find a reason to come back home.

One of those who did come back was LaVerne McGhee, who had left the community to pursue a nursing degree from Tulane University. She was drawn instinctively to a vocation of healing, for her father, Noah McGhee, was a medicine man. He gathered his herbs from the Alabama forests, and people came to him when they were sick, believing in the healing power of his touch and the Indian words that took away the pain. Even as she pursued her career, successfully, in New Orleans, Pensacola, and suburban Connecticut, LaVerne felt homesick for the place she had left. When she decided to return in the 1970s, she discovered that many things were still the same. There had always been a strong sense of community—people who were deeply attached to each other and shared a feeling of connection to their place. This was the heart of their identity.

But now there was more—better houses, paved roads, tribal enterprises to give people jobs—and a feeling of spiritual renewal as well. LaVerne discovered that at least once a month, Muscogee traditionalists gathered in a clearing deep in the woods to sing their songs in the ancestors' tongue and dance sometimes until it was almost dawn. And there was one more thing. With money from the Wind Creek casino, which opened in 2009, the tribe could offer college scholarships and other educational benefits—a full-circle affirmation of the Muscogee Education Movement and the struggles of Calvin McGhee and the elders.

All of it is part of McGhee's rich legacy.

His story is told, along with the broader history of the Muscogee people, in the Poarch Creek Indian Museum near the town of Atmore in Alabama. Once a year, tribal members gather at McGhee's grave, where the modest stone is chiseled with words from the twenty-third Psalm. "My family and I attend the graveside memorial annually," said tribal archivist Deidra Dees. "We have for many years. These are the stories we must keep alive. These are the stories of who we are."

The Slave Who Went to Congress

> This profile of the first African American from Alabama to serve in the U.S. Congress appeared in *Alabama Heritage*, and was later adapted into a children's book with the same title. It tells the story of a quest for racial justice and reconciliation by a man formerly enslaved, who possessed, I thought, way ahead of his time, the sensibilities of Dr. Martin Luther King Jr. and Nelson Mandela.

Benjamin Sterling Turner was born to a dark and turbulent history. Enslaved for the first forty years of his life, he was elected in 1870 to the U.S. House of Representatives. He was a man of towering eloquence, and became the first Black Alabamian to serve in Congress. In the end, his vision for the future and most of his proposed legislation were swept aside by the passions of the times. Indeed, Turner himself was lost to history until recent years, dismissed by many who, if they thought about him at all, saw him as simply an ineffective leader of Reconstruction.

During his lifetime, however, many of his white and Black constituents believed Ben Turner deserved a better fate. Finally, a few historians are catching up to that truth. Turner, who began his political career after the Civil War, embodied the hopes professed by Abraham Lincoln in his second Inaugural address, on March 4, 1865: "With malice toward none, with charity for all, with firmness in the right as God gives us to see the right, let us strive on to finish the work we are in, to bind up the nation's wounds, to care for him who shall have borne the battle and for his widow and his orphan, to do all which may achieve and cherish a just and lasting peace among ourselves and with all nations."

Turner, in his quest for public office, advocated for "universal suffrage and universal amnesty," by which he meant political equality for his fellow freedman but amnesty for whites who had fought for the Confederacy. "Let the past be forgotten," he declared, "and let us all, from every sun and every clime, of every hue and every shade, go to work peacefully to build up the shattered temples of this great and glorious Republic." Turner pursued his vision aggressively, though his story began in a very different time, far from Alabama in the coastal plains of North Carolina.

On March 17, 1825, he was born a slave in Halifax County, a strapping young man, in his teenage years, with copper-colored skin and ancestors that included whites, Blacks, and Native Americans. At the age of five, he moved to Alabama with his owner, Elizabeth Turner, and as he grew to adolescence, and then into adulthood, his character traits came quietly into focus.

From a young age, Turner was determined to educate himself. He learned to read despite the penalties a slave could face in pursuing that goal. After the Nat Turner Rebellion, which occurred at the time of Benjamin's move to Alabama, white slave owners across the South saw in the literate leader of that revolt a warning against the dangers of an educated slave. Benjamin Turner, however, seemed undeterred. According to one story handed down in his family, he had learned his rudimentary ABCs from an African American nurse who lived nearby. Other sources say his owner's children taught him to read. Whatever the case, the plantation overseer threatened Turner with lashes when he caught the young man studying a spelling book.

Sources disagree about the severity of the threat. Some say the overseer promised thirty-nine lashes, others five hundred. Either way, at the age of nineteen, Turner opted against open defiance, choosing instead to hide the spelling book and other reading materials, studying them only when he was alone.

Turner was, as one newspaper put it, "a man of splendid physique" and was well suited to the rigors of field work. His owners, however, chose to exploit the young man's intellect, and many of them soon granted him extraordinary responsibility. When Turner was in his twenties, his recently widowed owner sold the young slave to her stepdaughter's husband, Major W. H. Gee, who sought to help Elizabeth pay off debts with the money from the purchase. Gee was so impressed with his new manservant that he put him in charge of the Gee House Hotel, one of Selma's finest.

From all accounts, Turner ran the establishment effectively, quickly winning the respect of the owner. On January 8, 1857, in what was then a remarkable gesture, the Gee family hosted a wedding for Turner, presided over by the rector of St. Paul's Episcopal Church, perhaps the most prestigious white congregation in Selma. Turner's bride was a slave by the name of Independence, and according to some sources, the couple soon had a son they named Osceola. But their union quickly ended in heartbreak, for as Turner explained to an abolitionist friend from the North, Independence had "the fatal gift of beauty," and a white man bought her to be his mistress.

When Major Gee died, Turner's ownership transferred to another member of the family, Dr. James Gee. When the doctor went off to fight for the Confederacy, he left Turner in charge of another family hotel, the St. James, which was also regarded as one of Selma's best lodging establishments. With Gee's permission, Turner operated a livery stable on the side and began to amass his own modest fortune, at least by the standard of the times.

He carefully assessed the ebb and flow of the war, seeking to discern which side offered the best hope of emancipation. "I would have given my allegiance as readily to the Confederacy as to the United States," he later declared, "if the former, instead of the latter, had made me a free man."

As the fighting moved inexorably toward an end, it was clear that Turner's freedom would lie with the Union. But there was a heavy price to be paid. On April 2, 1865, the Northern forces under General James Wilson overran Selma and its important storehouse of Confederate munitions. As the Union cavalry laid waste to the town, burning more than two-thirds of it, Turner suffered as gravely as Selma's white citizens.

In testimony before the Southern Claims Commission, which considered the damage reports of civilians, Turner described what happened. "A squad of mounted men under command of an officer came to my stable and commenced taking out everything," he explained. "I had a very large, strong mule named Tom, to which I was much attached. He had become nearly blind. I asked them to leave me Tom, and after receiving hard words from them, the officer pointed his pistol at me and took him."

The Union cavalry, as Turner testified, also seized eight other mules and eight horses, plus 760 sacks of corn, fifty sacks of peas, and 118 "bales of fodder, averaging 415 pounds to the bale." But the indignity of it may have been the worst thing, for the soldiers also trampled Turner's garden, knocked down his fences, and tore up his barn. Not long afterward, he saw two of his horses—a mare and a colt—and one of his mules lying dead on the side of the road. "I was pleased enough at the taking of the town, and rejoiced until they took every thing I had," Turner said, "and then I got mad."

Perhaps that is why, when the war was over, Turner identified not only with his fellow freedmen, who had suffered the unspeakable brutality of slavery, but also with the plight of white Southerners. "They may have sinned wonderfully, but they suffered terribly," he proclaimed. "War was once the glory of her sons, but they paid the penalty for their offense, and for one, I have no coals of fiery reproach to heap upon them now. Rather would I extend the olive branch of peace."

For Turner, peace was the only course of action that made any sense, but he also knew that it would not be easy. In the months just after the end of the war, economic ruin hovered over the South—and with it the possibility of violence. Many former slaves, as an exercise of freedom, were flatly refusing to work in the fields, and white officials in Alabama and elsewhere were pushing a draconian set of "Black Codes," providing for the arrest of "vagrants" who would not go to work.

With tensions rising, Turner and a white doctor, John H. Henry, met with a group of restless freedmen and persuaded them to return to work—for pay this time—either in the fields of their former owners or for other employers who might need help. Whites appreciated Turner's stand and his outspoken efforts to promote racial peace, but it soon became clear that he also intended to argue the cause of Black suffrage.

In 1868, with the presidential election drawing near, Turner led a group of African Americans to meet with Judge William Brooks, a local leader in the Democratic Party and a firebrand for the cause of white supremacy. Turner proposed that the whites and Blacks of Selma work together and offered to cast his lot with the Democrats if Brooks and his party would support Black suffrage. "We refused," Brooks told the *Selma Times*, and instead he informed Turner and his followers that none of them deserved the right to vote because they did not know what to do with it. Turner immediately became a Republican.

In the presidential election of 1868, he supported the party nominee, Ulysses S. Grant, who, with Turner leading the local charge, carried Dallas County by 5,638 votes—almost exactly his margin of victory in Alabama. Nationally, Grant defeated Democrat Horatio Seymour by three hundred thousand votes, and as a president he supported Black voting rights, which he enforced by placing federal troops in the South.

Turner stepped forward to take advantage of that opportunity, sharing with many of his fellow freedmen the intoxicating hope that an era of political equality was at hand. In 1869 he was elected to Selma's City Council. He abruptly resigned after only nine months because the other councilmen voted to pay themselves a salary of twenty dollars a month, which Turner thought was wrong. As historian Alston Fitts later wrote, Turner "felt the city's financial plight was so desperate that councilmen should be willing to donate their time, effort, and influence." It was a stand respected by many of Selma's citizens, and the following year, riding a modest wave of popularity, Turner decided to run for the U.S. Congress.

In general, 1870 was a dangerous political year in Alabama for African Americans. In Sumter County, Richard Burke, a Black legislator, was murdered by whites who considered him extreme, while in Greene County the Ku Klux Klan killed four African Americans and wounded fifty-four at a political rally. Also, on an October night in Tuskegee, a white gunman stormed a meeting at the Zion Negro Church, killing two members and wounding three more. There were racial tensions in Selma as well, but Turner seemed immune. Even the *Selma Times*, a resolute supporter of white supremacy, hailed his entry into politics, saying, "His natural capacity is considerable; and in business and political matters his honesty is conceded." Running against Democrat Samuel Cumming, a white lawyer from neighboring Wilcox County, Turner eventually won the election by a vote of 18,226 to 16,461.

Soon after taking his congressional seat in March 1871, Turner introduced a bill to grant amnesty to all Confederate leaders, restoring their full political rights if they pledged their loyalty to the United States. Radical Republicans from other parts of the country, whose stance toward the South was far more punitive, made certain that Turner's bill died in committee. Back in Selma, however, his efforts drew praise from the city's white leaders. "He is a man of brains and will," declared former Confederate general Edmund Pettus, who would soon be elected to the U.S. Senate, "and he means to have his way."

At about the same time Turner also introduced a bill to restore St. Paul's Episcopal Church, one of many buildings destroyed by Union forces in 1865. In addition to paying for such repairs, Turner asked Congress to appropriate money to construct new federal buildings in Selma to help stimulate the local economy. He pleaded in Congress:

> In the year 1865, two-thirds of the city of Selma was reduced to ashes by

the United States Army. Churches, schoolhouses, manufactories, stores, workshops, public buildings, barns, stock pens, and a thousand or more private residences were swept away by the destroying flames. In short, nearly the whole city was burned. The Government made a display in that unfortunate city of its mighty power and conquered a gallant and high-toned people.... I now ask Congress, in behalf of the people of that ruined city, to be as bountiful toward them in mercy as the Army was vigorous and ambitious in reducing them to subjugation.

For those who might question Turner's aggressive representation of Selma's white citizens—the former slave masters of African Americans like himself—his answer was simple: "The people of Selma have been magnanimous toward me," he said, "I intend to stand by to labor for them in their need and desolation."

Turner also labored for his fellow freedmen. Even before his election to Congress, he donated land and money for the construction of Black schools in Selma. Once in Washington, he supported integrated schools and Black voting rights, helped secure a pension for African American soldiers who had fought for the Union, and introduced two sweeping pieces of legislation that, if passed, would have helped build an economic foundation for destitute African American farmers.

Turner asked first of all for the refunding of a cotton tax levied on the South just after the war. It was a tax, he said, that fell hardest on the people least able to pay—the workers in the fields, particularly the recently liberated slaves. "Now, I plead in behalf of the poor people of the South, regardless of caste or color," Turner declared, "because this tax had its blighting influence. It cut the jugular vein of our financial system, bled it near to death."

In the same speech, Turner asked Congress to go even further, setting aside federal money to buy up land and sell it inexpensively to poor farmers of the South, especially former slaves:

> I ask Congress to make this appropriation, and I ask it in behalf of the landless and poor people of our country. In that section of the country that I have the honor in part to represent upon this floor the people are extremely poor, having been emancipated from slavery after hundreds of years of disappointment and privation. These people have struggled longer and labored harder, and have made more of the raw material than any people in the world.... They are laboring and making every effort to secure land and houses. It is next to impossible that this generation will accomplish it without such aid as I now ask from the Government.

This was, in effect, a call for reparations—not a giveaway, but a government investment in the economic well-being of its newest citizens. One of the bitter truths of Reconstruction is that the government never answered such a call. For many of those who were formerly enslaved, the dream of economic independence gave way to a system of tenancy and sharecropping almost as oppressive as slavery itself. The hope of freedom disappeared as well, as white Southerners over the next thirty years rallied behind the political maneuvering of the Democratic Party, and the terrorism of the Ku Klux Klan, to disenfranchise African Americans.

Turner watched it all with dismay. In 1872 he lost his bid for reelection when another Black candidate ran against him. Philip Joseph, a highly educated African American newspaper editor from Mobile, regarded the self-taught Turner as "a man destitute of education" and thought the voters deserved something better. Joseph ran a distant third in the election but managed to siphon off enough Black votes to give the victory to a white Mobilian, Frederick Bromberg.

Benjamin Turner remained intermittently active in politics, serving as a delegate to the Republican National Convention in 1880, and also as a presidential elector, but he eventually retired to private life. According to a family biography written by his brother-in-law, Jackson Todd, whose education Turner had supported financially, the former Congressman "purchased a 640 acre farm," where he raised cotton, corn, and oats. His last years, however, would not be easy.

Turner faced bankruptcy during the economic downturn of the late 1870s, and his farm was sold to pay off his debts. He died in poverty in 1894, and when the *Selma Times* took note of his passing, the obituary was couched in the racial condescension of the time: "Ben was not a bad man at heart, but was on the contrary a good negro, and was liked by everybody. He was exceedingly courteous to every one and while drawing a salary of a congressman never for a moment forgot his position or presumed upon his office to force himself into the presence of his superiors."

If not for the efforts of Alston Fitts, a historian who worked for the Catholic Church, Turner's legacy might have ended with his death and burial in an unmarked grave in Selma's Old Live Oak Cemetery. Fitts came to Selma in 1978 and took a job with the Edmundite order, where Father Paul Morin urged him to research Turner's story. Fitts pored through newspaper files and Congressional records, and eventually he located Turner's grave. He helped put together a biracial committee to erect a monument on the site, next to a small crape myrtle tree. Turner, Fitts wrote in the *Selma Times-Journal*, "deserves that much." Out of Fitts's efforts has come a reconsideration of Turner's life, a realization among some historians that Turner was a man ahead of his time—a tireless proponent of economic progress, racial peace, and political equality for African Americans.

It was, at the time, a vision at odds with American history. In the years just after the Civil War, there was, in the final analysis, too much hurt and hate in the air.

Footnote: The Forgotten Statesman

This vignette is excerpted from an article that appeared in *Alabama Heritage*.

If Benjamin Turner has begun to receive the historical recognition he deserves, that is not the case with the second Black Congressman from Alabama, James T. Rapier. Elected in 1872 from a district in the northern part of the state, Rapier quickly established himself as one of the most distinguished statesmen in the U.S. House of Representatives.

His life was very different from Turner's. For one thing he was never enslaved. He was born free in Florence, Alabama, the son of a prosperous African American barber. And if Turner, for all his eloquence, was self-educated, Rapier studied at some of the finest schools in the world. At the age of five, he moved from Alabama to Nashville, where he lived with his paternal grandmother and soon began his formal education.

Later, he would travel with a family member to Buxton, Ontario, Canada, where he became part of a community of African Americans who had escaped from slavery. He studied for a time at the Buxton Mission School before earning his teaching degree in Toronto. Soon he continued his education at the University of Glasgow in Scotland, then returned to Canada to study law at Montreal College.

He was admitted to the bar and almost certainly could have built a prosperous life for himself, safely removed from the racial turmoil in America. Instead, he returned to Alabama at the end of the Civil War and threw himself into Reconstruction politics. He was elected to Congress at a time of rising political violence and became a target of threats from the Ku Klux Klan as he pursued the cause of racial equality.

His passion was the Civil Rights Act of 1875, legislation that would have had sweeping implications if it had ever been enforced. It outlawed discrimination in public accommodations and travel, public schools and jury selection, and even forbade the segregation of cemeteries. It passed in 1875, partly because of Rapier's support. But in 1883 the U.S. Supreme Court declared it unconstitutional.

Rapier already was deeply disillusioned. Klan violence was turning deadly in Alabama with the assassination of a Black state legislator, a mass shooting at a church in Tuskegee, and an attack on a political rally in Greene County that killed four African Americans and wounded fifty-four.

In the face of that reality and with the impending end of Reconstruction, Rapier urged his fellow Black citizens to emigrate west of the Mississippi River, and bought his own parcel of land in Kansas. But he never lived there. In 1883, he fell ill and died nearly penniless in Montgomery. In Alabama today, almost nobody knows his name.

But there is also this. Rapier vowed early in his political career never to support any legislation, or compromise with any political system, that failed to acknowledge his standing "as a man." From childhood on, he understood what it meant to be free. For the rest of his life, this was a nonnegotiable demand.

Epilogue

In 1964, some eighty years after Rapier's death, the main provisions of the civil rights legislation he helped to shape were incorporated into the Civil Rights Act of 1964, the most consequential legislation of its kind ever passed by the U.S. Congress. This was Rapier's most important legacy—his role in the struggle to keep the idea of equality alive.

The Story of a Typewriter

This account, published in *Mobile Bay Magazine*, was also part of the catalogue for an exhibition, "A History of Mobile in 22 Objects," at the History Museum of Mobile.

It was the kind of scene a cub reporter doesn't soon forget, the front of the house caved in by a bomb and its owner standing calmly in the yard, a Band-Aid above one eye, speaking to one or two city officials who had come that morning to offer their condolences. John LeFlore, Mobile's most prominent civil rights leader, had been working the night before, on June 27, 1967, at the manual typewriter he kept in the kitchen. It was his weapon of choice in a crusade for justice going back at least to 1925.

Around midnight, he went to bed and was sleeping soundly at 1:33 a.m. when a powerful explosion ripped through the house. He thought at first it might be the air conditioner in the living room but realized immediately it was something much worse. This was not the only attempt on his life. In 1969, a bomb on his front porch failed to explode, and five years before that a gunman had fired shots into his home. This time it was close. The night before the bombing, LeFlore had worked at his typewriter until two in the morning. If that had been the case on June 27, almost certainly LeFlore would have died.

As a young reporter covering the scene, I remember the eerie morning silence, a few hushed murmurs between LeFlore and a small group of well-wishers, and the horrifying damage to the five-room house at 1504 Chatague Avenue. But the most unforgettable thing was the stoic composure of LeFlore himself. He had seen a lot since 1925, when he began his personal quest for civil rights, and I was struck that morning by his quiet, almost matter-of-fact affirmation that there was still a lot of work to be done.

He had been inspired to take a stand sometime early in the 1920s, when he was riding one evening on a Mobile trolley—a Black teenager minding his own business—and a surly white man demanded his seat. The two of them argued, then began to scuffle, and when the police were called, LeFlore was arrested and the white man went free. Affronted by the patent injustice, LeFlore vowed that he would be the one to set things right. In 1925, he set out to revitalize Mobile's chapter of the NAACP. For the next fifty years, under the auspices of that organization, and later Mobile's Non-Partisan Voters League, he worked every day for the cause of civil rights.

Armed with his typewriter, he documented lynchings, demanded equal access by African Americans to the wartime industries springing up in Mobile, protested mistreatment of Blacks on city buses, and, most importantly, crusaded for greater access to the ballot. He found a white ally in Joseph Langan, who, as a state legislator in the 1940s, staunchly opposed a constitutional amendment to make it harder for African Americans in Alabama to vote.

Later, as a city commissioner, Langan worked with LeFlore to address the most obvious examples of segregation—the buses, the public library, the police—and Mobile developed a reputation in the South as a place of racial moderation. But by the 1960s, more militant African Americans were becoming impatient with what they saw as the slow rate of progress. Supporters of an organization called NOW (Neighborhood Organized Workers) blamed the gradualism on LeFlore, and some even called him an Uncle Tom. There were rumors, in fact, that the perpetrator of the bombing in 1967 may have been Black.

No one, Black or white, was ever charged.

Despite the attempt on his life and continuing opposition from conservative whites—and now from more radical African Americans—LeFlore kept pushing. In 1975, only a few months before his death from a heart attack, he worked with longtime activist ally Wiley Bolden on what became perhaps the most lasting legacy of the Mobile movement—a lawsuit demanding a more representative city government. Until then, Mobile's three-person city commission, which was elected at large, had been all white. LeFlore and Bolden, who became lead plaintiff in the case, argued that the exclusion of Blacks from the commission was both deliberate and inevitable in a city that was still majority white.

U.S. district judge Virgil Pittman ruled in their favor, but city officials appealed and a bitter controversy ensued. Finally, in 1982 the legal maneuvering ran its course, and Mobile adopted a new mayor-council government with districts that assured it would be interracial. In the new political environment, still contentious, but now more inclusive, not only has the council been an integrated body, but Mobile elected its first Black mayor, Sam Jones, who served two terms.

Some have argued that there is no better symbol of Mobile's struggles and racial progress than a manual typewriter once owned by LeFlore. Nor is there a more powerful reminder of all the work that remains to be done.

Books That Matter

These essays on books that touched my heart, or made me think, were written, respectively, for the Alabama Writers Forum, *Salvation South, Chapter 16,* and the *Alabama Review.*

The Last Slave Ship

Our grief so heavy look lak we cain stand it. I think maybe I die in my sleep when I dream about my mama.
—Cudjo Lewis

On April 10, 2018, a diver slipped into the murky waters of the river delta north of Mobile. Spring floods had stirred the muddy bottom, and the water, he remembered, "looked like chocolate milk." Even with his scuba mask, Ben Raines was diving blind. Soon, his foot brushed against what felt like a wooden plank, and Raines, a heralded environmental reporter, reached down and began to tug. The plank came loose, and he rose to the surface with a five-foot piece of what turned out to be the *Clotilda*, the last slave ship to arrive in America.

Now Raines has written a powerful book about the history of that ship, a legacy of oppression, bravery, and environmental injustice—and, he hopes, of redemption. The story began with a fateful bet by an Alabama riverboat captain named Tim Maeher.

In April 1859, Maeher and some of the passengers were discussing the future of slavery. As a proslavery zealot, Maeher chafed against the effects of a fifty-year-old law banning the importation of slaves from Africa—a piece of legislation, he knew, that was driving up the price of human chattel sold within the boundaries of the United States. It was a simple matter of supply and demand. Maeher, becoming more animated, placed a bet with his passengers that he could skirt the law and import more Africans, thus doing his part to increase the supply and drive down the price. The Southern economy deserved no less.

He commissioned the *Clotilda* and hired a man named William Foster to captain the vessel on its transatlantic voyage. In telling the story of what happened next, Raines pays careful tribute to four women writers—Emma Langdon Roche, Zora Neale Hurston, Natalie

Robertson, and Sylviane Diouf—who kept the story of the *Clotilda* alive. Of those writers, Hurston, perhaps, painted the most vivid portrait of the slave trade, a brutal reality with its roots in Africa. A native Alabamian raised in Florida, Hurston is best-known in literary history for her iconic Harlem Renaissance novel *Their Eyes Were Watching God*. But she was a young folklorist in 1927 when she began to interview Cudjo Lewis, the last survivor of the *Clotilda* voyage.

In multiple conversations, sometimes prodded by gifts of peaches, watermelon, or ham, Lewis offered an idyllic picture of his African upbringing, interrupted brutally when he was a young man of nineteen. That was 1860, the year when an army of warriors from the African kingdom of Dahomey descended on his village, led by a shock troop of women fighters. Based on Cudjo's conversations with Hurston, Raines describes the dreadful attack: "Cudjo says the killing came so fast that the elderly who tried to flee were caught as soon as they emerged from their homes. All around, headless bodies, young and old, poured blood into the streets. The air was filled with the iron stench of blood, and with screaming, from both the dying and the war cries of the Amazons marauding through the streets."

As Hurston herself later wrote about the horrible truth of Cudjo's account—a truth that applied to millions of those sentenced to the impossible cruelties of slavery—"the inescapable fact that stuck in my craw was: my people had *sold* me and the white people had bought me.... It impressed upon me the universal nature of greed and glory."

There *is* a measure of glory in *The Last Slave Ship*. It comes on the other side of enslavement, a fate that the 110 *Clotilda* captives endured for five years—from 1860 until the end of the Civil War. Cudjo is clear about those brutalities, including the dreaded Middle Passage across the Atlantic in the hold of a vessel barely ninety feet long. For five years after their arrival, the Africans worked in the fields from before the sun rose until after it set. "But we don't grieve about dat," said Cudjo. "We cry 'cause we slave."

When freedom came, many of the *Clotilda* captives settled in a swampy area along the Mobile River. "Almost immediately," wrote Raines, "in an extraordinary act of self-governance, the group began to build a community for themselves ruled by the social strictures they had grown up with." For a time, Africa Town flourished. By the 1920s, it had grown to a community of fifteen hundred, one of the largest in the nation governed by African Americans. By the 1970s, the population had reached twelve thousand—"shady streets," as Raines described it, "lined with tidy wood-frame and brick houses and home to a vibrant commercial district."

Even during this remarkable period that lasted for more than a hundred years, the story was not without pain. The forces of segregation and disenfranchisement affected African Americans all over the South. But the fall of Africa Town lay, ultimately, in environmental pollution so intense that cancers of multiple kinds began to ravage the community. As Raines explained, chemicals from heavy industry, including two paper mills on the edge of the community, "are linked to cancer, birth defects, fertility problems, kidney and liver damage, nose and throat irritation, asthma, and loss of hearing and color vision."

Year after year, toxic ash puffed from the stacks of the paper mills, drifting down like snow (though one resident said the falling debris reminded him more of "rodent droppings"). Residents were forced to wash their cars every day to keep the paint from peeling off. They complained, wrote Raines, "but because they came from an African-American community in rigidly segregated Alabama, no one in a position of power listened to the complaints."

Inevitably, the population has declined. Vacant lots scar the landscape. Raines, however, ends his evocative narrative—so full of cruelty and sadness, with a history of heroism in between—on a note of hope. He believes his discovery of the sunken ship, since confirmed by marine archeologists, has begun to trigger a spirit of reconciliation. A descendant of Captain William Foster recently visited Africatown asking forgiveness from the *Clotilda* families. And in the African nation of Benin, where two tribes—heirs to the enslavers and the enslaved—share the same land, there are efforts to reach across the divide.

In the course of his research, Raines traveled to Benin, where he interviewed Pastor Romain Zannou, leader of his country's reconciliation movement. "I believe this can take place on a larger scale," Zannou told Raines.

> And it must. People who think that slavery is all sins of the past, no need for reconciliation, I think there is evidence in America that this is not true, that the sin is happening yesterday and today, not centuries ago. You see that when something happens to an African American, shot by mistake by a white police officer, you see it come back, that sin and the

pain it causes, full strength again. It is there on the faces. There are those who want to ignore it, because reconciliation is not an easy path. If it were, it would have happened a long time ago. But it must be our path.

For many of the heirs to the *Clotilda* saga, this is the hope, the possibility of redemption, contained in the story of the last slave ship. No one believes that it will be easy. Given the racial climate of the country, including the city where the *Clotilda* landed, it may well be an improbable hope. But there has been a critical mass of interest. Raines's book is one of four published since 2007, and the internationally acclaimed film *Descendant*, directed by Mobile native Margaret Brown, has provided a haunting oral history—voices of men and women raised on stories, often told in whispers, of bravery and suffering among the *Clotilda* captives.

"I was told that's why I was born—to know this story," concluded Emmett Lewis, a descendant of Cudjo. "My only fear is for my people's story not to be told."

As one of the storytellers, Ben Raines shares that sense of urgency. "It's the origin story for the African diaspora," he says. "It's the experience of African Americans in America, all in one six-square-mile community."

Fugitives of the Heart

Yates, the protagonist, was just a boy when his daddy was killed, shot for stealing a side of meat from a neighbor in the hills of Tennessee. Times are hard for the characters who populate William Gay's latest book, the last in a string of posthumous novels pieced together by his friends from an attic full of scenes that Gay left behind. The writing, as always, was exquisite. For Michael White and the others who figured out how the scenes fit together, the effort was worth it, this forensic labor of a love they feel even now for a writer who died in 2012. William Gay, they will tell you, was one of a kind; more precisely, he was a once-in-a-generation talent who could read the works of Mark Twain, William Faulkner, or Cormac McCarthy, absorb what they were trying to do, then do it himself and make it his own.

Fugitives of the Heart is Gay's homage to Twain. Yates is Huck Finn in a different century, a boy of battered nobility and heart, hard around the edges and living off the land, whose only real friend is a Black man getting by on the margins of the segregated South. This is the *rough South*, the hills and hollows of Appalachia, where the Depression came early and never went away and people just did the best they could. Some of them anyway. But maybe not Yates's daddy, whose body was dumped from the back of a wagon by the man who caught him stealing from the smokehouse. The killer also left the side of meat: *If he wanted it bad enough to trade his life for it then it's hisn*. For the boy it was almost more than he could bear, but the mountains turned pretty in the spring, "a warm wind looping up from the south," and Yates took heart: "He saw this early spring as a gift from the fates. A balancing of some cosmic scale. The scent of wildflower rode the winds and he moved through this Edenic world with a newfound confidence. He began to think he might make it after all."

I came late to the work of William Gay, to novels such as *The Long*

Home and *Provinces of Night* or the short story collection *I Hate to See That Evening Sun Go Down*. I was astonished by his literary gift—and after I learned it, almost as much by his biography. To many readers, his story is familiar; to others, not at all, even after all this time. But this was the heart of it. Gay was born in 1941, growing up white in poverty so extreme that for many of us, it is hard to imagine—a family with no car, living in a house with no electricity, lit at night by a kerosene lamp. Gay developed a hard sense of the South, a geography of the heart that he shared with writers such as Rick Bragg, Larry Brown, and Tim McLaurin.

But there was also this. As Gay became a voracious reader, inspired by the words of Flannery O'Connor and William Faulkner, he discovered that he understood—technically, artistically—exactly what they were doing. He also discovered he could do it too. In his twenties, he began to write almost full-time, eschewing other jobs unless the wolf was at the door, and "by age thirty-five," says Michael White, "he had honed his style and was at the height of his powers, and he knew it. But . . . no one was buying."

Gay was fifty-nine before anything he wrote was published, accumulating a stack of rejections that would make most writers wither. When I read this, I thought of my friend, the Nashville nonfiction writer John Egerton, who used to paper his bathroom wall with rejection letters from New York publishers. For Egerton, it was a wry and self-effacing way of poking fun, of maintaining his own equilibrium. But his rejections began to subside long before they did for William Gay. I asked White how he thought Gay did it. What kept him going?

"The short answer," White replied, "is William was a born writer, there was nothing else in his life that mattered from the time he was a teenager on; it was discouraging to him, but his destiny as a writer was written in the stars and he had no choice but to obey regardless of the consequences; it was his life, and he had to do it regardless of whether anyone was reading it or not."

In a postscript to *Fugitives of the Heart*, White wrote about the first time he visited Gay and they were talking about Cormac McCarthy. Gay urged White to read McCarthy's *Suttree* and White reported that he was "blown away"—not only by McCarthy's exquisite language but also by his ability, as White put it, "to make readers aware of events without ever describing them in the text." It was an artful literary device that White could see in Gay's own writing. When they talked about it, Gay smiled.

The prototype, he said, could be found in Faulkner's *The Hamlet*. Such had been Gay's study of the craft, the literary *art*, that he detected in other writers and incorporated into his work.

He loved to talk about his favorites, almost to revel in his own admiration ("he was one of the most humble writers I'd ever met," said his publisher, Joe Taylor, of Livingston Press), and in *Fugitives of the Heart*, Gay lets his central character find words for his respect. Late in the novel, Yates, the boy, reflects on life with the widow Paiton:

> Nights by the fire she'd read to him Biblical tales. The stories of stern old prophets, their mad ravings. . . . She'd temper this with Twain, a chapter a night of Huckleberry Finn, Jim and Huck in a fix on the sunrimpled Mississippi. He could almost smell the hot torpor of the river, seeing the country sliding past, until he was hopelessly snared by Twain, forced to seek out the book in surreptitious moments during the day, finishing the book far ahead of her, though she pretended not to notice and went on reading his chapter a night anyway.

Ultimately, of course, *Fugitives of the Heart* is not *Adventures of Huckleberry Finn*, nor is it merely an echo set in another time. It is not as funny, for one thing. Its humor takes the form of irony, and while it is written in third person, not first, Gay has a gift for point of view, reflecting the world through the eyes of a ragamuffin boy, while still managing, as Twain did, to write in scenes that are lyrical and lovely—almost as if he were painting with words. But the portrait is dark. The interracial friendship at the heart of the story, which seems so promising at the start—flintier, perhaps, than the relationship between Jim and Huck, but a bulwark against a hard world—abruptly takes on the specter of betrayal. Redemption comes at a terrible cost, more in the form of authentic survival, and we are left with the unmistakable sense that this is the best that Yates can hope for.

Or the rest of us, for that matter: "They had moved across the earth as briefly as the passage of the sun, then they were gone and all there was to mark their tenancy were random hieroglyphics, senseless and insignificant as a chicken's scratching in the dust. Then the wind rose and that was gone too." But Gay is also telling us, through his life and the body of his writing—more perhaps than in any single work—that there *have* to be the stories. Otherwise, the emptiness is too much to endure.

Atticus Finch
The Biography

In *Atticus Finch: The Biography*, Joseph Crespino has given us a brilliant, readable historian's rumination on the making of a literary icon. How did Harper Lee conceive of Atticus? What were the subtle ties in her own understanding of this most iconic of fictional characters, and how did Atticus capture our hearts and imagination as he did?

These are the questions Crespino addresses, and I was surprised at the depth of personal reflection this book prompted. I was thirteen when my father gave me a copy of *To Kill a Mockingbird*. This was 1960 and the book had just appeared, and in my own Alabama family—with roots in the county where Harper Lee was born—*Mockingbird* carried its share of controversy. One of my aunts refused to read it, so offended was she by its revelations of racial injustice.

My father was a different story. Like Atticus, he was a lawyer who believed that the courts, alone among human institutions, were "the great leveler," and when he was elected as a circuit judge in the year of *Mockingbird*'s publication, he had promised Black voters that his courtroom would be colorblind. But in our family all of this was a delicate dance, for my father was also a segregationist, deeply invested in the status quo.

As Crespino reminds us, this was also true of Atticus. We know this because Harper Lee told us so, not so much in *Mockingbird*, though there were intimations of paternalism, but in her second book, *Go Set a Watchman*, which she had actually written first. Atticus is older in *Watchman*, and to the horror of many American readers, he is not as likeable the second time around. As Crespino writes, "Atticus, though physically weakened, is still wry, lively, and loving. The novel turns when Jean Louise discovers a racist, right-wing book among his reading materials. She heads immediately to the county courthouse where Atticus . . . had gone to a meeting. Looking on from the balcony, she discovers that it is a gathering of the White Citizens' Council. The rest of the novel tracks her outrage and disbelief that her wise and loving father would take up with such bigoted malcontents."

Crespino makes a strong case that personal experiences for Harper Lee shaped the dual character of Atticus. If, as most biographers assume, her father A. C. Lee was one of the prototypes for Atticus, A. C.'s career as a small-town newspaper editor foreshadowed the depiction of Finch in both of Lee's novels. Crespino pores through the untapped trove of editorials in the *Monroe Journal*, which A. C. owned and edited for two decades. What he finds is a patrician idealist who believed in the law and good order and, among other things, hated the Southern practice of lynching.

These ritualized killings were still widespread in the 1930s when Lee began his editorship of the *Journal*, and as he knew from his time as a lawyer, they sometimes enjoyed the cover of the courts. Lee once represented two Black men accused of murdering a white man, and one of the victim's sons was a member of the jury. Despite Lee's objections, the verdict was swift and his clients were hung. A few years later a Black man accused of raping and murdering a white woman was kidnapped from a small-town jail about forty miles south of Monroeville. Crespino describes what happened next: "They took him to an alternate location and murdered him, but not before subjecting him to two hours of sadistic torture, including castration, forced autocannibalism, stabbing, burning with hot irons, and dismemberment of toes and fingers. They tied [his] body to the back of a car."

A. C. Lee hated such moments of barbarism and carried stories on the front page of the *Journal* about the grand jury investigation that followed. But when Northern members of Congress proposed antilynching bills in response, first in 1935, and again in 1938, Lee editorialized against the legislation. This was, he thought, an infringement on self-governance in the South. When Harper Lee began writing *Go Set a Watchman* early in 1957, her book became a dialogue between a young woman like herself, concerned with the burden of racial injustice, and a father who accepted white supremacy, cloaked by the cover of states' rights.

Jean Louise Finch, the woman in the story, loves her father, just as the author of the novel loved hers. Both fathers, after all, were intelligent, gentle, and loving, and the struggle in *Watchman* was to try and understand how the pieces fit together. The novel, at first, was rejected.

As Crespino notes, Harper Lee's editors at Lippincott found it lacking a sense of story. But they also recognized her talent, and when they urged her to try again, the book that emerged was *To Kill a Mockingbird*. It did not come easily or quickly. But when it was published in 1960, the character of Atticus was very different. He was a single father, first and foremost, raising two young children with wisdom and patience, even as he accepted the unpopular duty of representing a Black man accused of rape. In the *Mockingbird* casting of Atticus, Ms. Lee removed the less pleasant qualities revealed in *Watchman*, and we encounter instead a Southern white man both honorable and decent in taking his stand against injustice. Crespino argues that Atticus grew even nobler in the movie portrayal by Gregory Peck.

In the course of the whole creative process, the author and the actor gave the country—and especially the South—something many of us needed to see: a white man trying to do the right thing. As I read the book on multiple occasions, I saw something different in it every time; the adventure story I read at thirteen became by the time I finished high school a moral affirmation of the power of decency to guide us through the turbulent 1960s.

I found myself thinking about my grandfather, who did, in fact, resemble Atticus Finch. Both versions of him. Samuel Palmer Gaillard was the family patriarch who lived to be 103. He was born in 1856 and died in 1959, and so, remarkably, he remembered the Civil War and lived through the beginnings of the civil rights movement. Like Atticus, he was a patrician—a man of gentle and tolerant wisdom, steeped in the culture of his place; a lawyer who was proud of having represented Black clients and having never lost a case on their behalf; who defended in public the integrationist sermons of the beloved young minister at his church, but argued with the minister in private about the wisdom of segregation, before conceding on his deathbed: "Pastor, I see now that you were right."

As I absorbed the lessons of *To Kill a Mockingbird*, which seemed at its heart to be a novel about empathy and justice, I hoped that the trajectory of my grandfather's life, culminating in his moment of redemption, might be the trajectory of his beloved South—indeed, of the country. Others shared that hope. In *Atticus Finch: The Biography*, Crespino writes about Martin Luther King Jr. and the promise and power he saw in the novel—in King's words, the "the force of moral courage" he hoped might guide the good white people of America. To which Crespino adds:

It was to them [white people] that [Harper Lee] had written a novel that would eventually be read and celebrated around the world as a timeless expression of universal values of moral courage, tolerance, and understanding. But she began the project confused and uncertain. In her first attempt at writing a novel, she had wanted to reconcile her abiding love and respect for her father with the hypocrisy and injustice that he and his generation of southerners had too easily abided, all while defending him from the condescension of northern liberals. Yet through that process, and shaped, too, by the shifting politics of the day, she stumbled upon a simpler narrative: a father, inspired by his love and hope for his children, doing the right thing in a time of crisis. In that story, Atticus rose to the occasion.

But time moves on, and in the bleaker unfolding of the American story—the durability of our original sin—Harper Lee's *Watchman*, rejected by her publisher at the time she wrote it, saw the light of day in 2015, just a few months before she died. Suddenly, we were forced to see Atticus in a different way, for even though *Watchman* was written first, it was a sequel to the story of *To Kill a Mockingbird*. Atticus, we were startled to learn, had not grown wiser with time. He could still be gentle, loving, and kind, but he was also, much like the South in which he lived, still a racist deep in his heart.

This larger, darker, more complicated truth, revealed in the pages of both her novels, is the legacy—and the greatness—of Harper Lee.

Sidney Poitier
"We'll Catch a Later Plane"

> This reminiscence was written for the online magazine *Chapter 16*. It is based in part on an article written more than fifty years earlier for my student newspaper, the *Vanderbilt Hustler*.

January 6, 2022, was a day of multilayered sadness. Not only was it the first anniversary of an insurrection—the deadly attack on the U.S. Capitol—it was also the day Sidney Poitier died.

With this passing of an American icon, my friend Hugh Moore shared a treasure I had forgotten—an article I had written in the *Vanderbilt Hustler*, our student newspaper, about a visit Poitier made to Fisk University. The date was 1966, the hundredth anniversary of Fisk, and Poitier and his friend Harry Belafonte were the centennial speakers.

As *Hustler* editor, Hugh had suggested that he and I cover the event. We had seen Poitier's most recent movie, *A Patch of Blue*, and we understood—how could we not?—the cultural relevance of his career. In films like *Lilies of the Field*, *A Raisin in the Sun*, and now his latest, Poitier embodied a reality he thought America must see—a Black man of dignity and strength. Three films would follow in 1967—*In the Heat of the Night*, which won the Academy Award for Best Picture, *To Sir with Love*, and *Guess Who's Coming to Dinner*, all of which dealt head-on with the enduring legacy of racial segregation.

By the time of his visit to Fisk, Poitier was well on his way to becoming one of the most popular actors in the country. Belafonte was as legendary for his support of the civil rights movement as he was for his calypso singing. Hugh and I were a little starstruck. We were also surprised when the two celebrities agreed to be interviewed, even briefly, by a couple of white guys from the student newspaper across town.

The interview itself was uninspiring. We asked something about the role of universities in American life, and Poitier replied, "Art cannot survive without the full support of universities, which are the center of culture." Maybe if there had been more time, he would have talked about Fisk University in particular, for most assuredly he knew its story.

He understood, as his speech made clear, that as soon as the Civil War was over, abolitionists from the American Missionary Society were traveling the South, making their plans for what came next after the abolition of slavery. Many of these were white men, such as John Ogden, Erastus Milo Cravath, and Edward Parmelee, the founders of Fisk, who worked with the assistant commissioner of the Freedman's Bureau, Clinton B. Fisk, to secure a former military barracks as the site for a school.

Classes began on January 9, 1866, and within a few months enrollment had soared to nine hundred students. For the next hundred years Fisk stood as a symbol of Black aspiration, and by the civil rights years, many of its students were leaders in the movement. Two of the most prominent were Diane Nash and John Lewis, who had transferred to Fisk from American Baptist Theological Seminary.

April 19, 1960, was a watershed day. Early that morning, a bomb exploded at the home of Z. Alexander Looby, an African American attorney who represented students arrested during Nashville's lunch counter sit-ins. So powerful was the blast that Looby's house was nearly destroyed. Down the street at Meharry Medical College, more than 140 windows were shattered, and dozens of people were cut by the glass.

Miraculously, neither Looby nor his wife was hurt. But outrage swept through the Black community, and the students decided to march in protest. In what would become a defining image of the decade, the ranks of the marchers swelled to several thousand as they walked in silence toward city hall. Nashville mayor Ben West waited for them on the steps.

At first the mayor seemed nervous and defensive, but Diane Nash approached him calmly. Speaking with resolve, she asked if West would use his office to end discrimination in Nashville.

"I appeal to all citizens to end discrimination," he replied, "to have no bigotry, no bias, no hatred."

"Then, Mayor," insisted Nash, continuing to push, "do you recommend that lunch counters be desegregated?"

"Yes," said West.

It was a moment of triumph for the civil rights movement, one that resonated throughout the South. Thus, at Fisk's centennial celebration, it was more than a cliché when Harry Belafonte said of its students, "The future of America rests in their hands."

Looking back on it now, that is the dominant memory Hugh Moore and I carry from that day—the extraordinary level of mutual respect between two Black celebrities and the students they had come to address. In our article for the student newspaper, we wrote, "The two stars spoke to a packed house in the Fisk Auditorium . . . then greeted students informally at a reception that afternoon. . . . For more than three hours they signed autographs and conversed about any subject from the weather to civil rights."

When a Fisk official informed the entertainers that it was time to go, that their plane was scheduled to leave in thirty minutes, Poitier replied, "No, we'll catch a later plane."

It occurred to me then, as it has since, that this simple display of humanity—the clear priorities of a cultural hero—may have been the most memorable lesson of that unforgettable day.

"Thank God, a Young Person Had a Camera"

> These reflections on contemporary headlines—heroism wrapped in brutality and violence—were adapted from multiple Facebook posts.

1.

I first learned her name on the night of May 29, 2020, four days after her video went viral. By now we had watched it multiple times—transfixed by the horrifying nine minutes, a policeman with his knee on a Black man's neck, gazing with a kind of reptilian menace in the general direction of the camera, while the life drained out of the body beneath him. We had listened in shock to the victim's pleas, his desperate cries that he could not breathe, and finally we heard him call out for his mama.

We knew by now that his name was George Floyd. We knew the killer's name was Derek Chauvin. But many of us had not thought to ask who exactly had made the video, who had had the presence of mind to leave us unable to shrug off the truth. On *The Last Word*, his late evening show on MSNBC, Lawrence O'Donnell gave us the answer. It was a seventeen-year-old girl.

"The full truth of this story can only be told," O'Donnell declared, in what sounded like hyperbole, but was not, "because of the heroism of a seventeen-year-old girl, Darnella Frazier. . . . She pushed 'record' on her phone and she stood there and held her ground for ten minutes."

Later we would learn the details of her story—how on the evening of May 25 she was caring for her nine-year-old cousin when they decided to go to the convenience store. As they were approaching Cup Foods, maybe two or three storefronts away, Darnella noticed four Minneapolis policemen dragging a Black man from the back of a car. As she and her cousin drew closer, she saw an officer kneeling on the man's neck and heard him begging for his life: "I can't breathe." Twenty-seven times he would say it.

A crowd gathered. Darnella sent her cousin into the store and pulled out her phone. She had seen this kind of thing before. As she aimed her camera at Derek Chauvin, who was only a few feet away, Chauvin stared back. At one point he reached for his mace.

"I felt in danger when he did that," she said.

Her lawyer, Seth Cobin, affirmed that his client was "utterly terrified. . . . But she knew that without this record the world would never know what happened that day. . . . She had no idea she would witness and document one of the most important and high-profile police murders in American history. If it wasn't for her bravery, presence of mind, and steady hand, and her willingness to post the video on Facebook and share her trauma with the world, all four of those police officers would still be on the streets, possibly terrorizing other members of the community."

Cobin said Frazier wasn't looking to be a hero. She was, instead, "just a seventeen-year-old high school student, with a boyfriend and a job at the mall, who did the right thing. She's the Rosa Parks of her generation."

As a journalist-historian who came of age during the civil rights years, I could understand why Cobin would say that. But I thought there was a better comparison. Nine months before Rosa Parks refused to relinquish her seat on a Montgomery bus, a teenager in that city had done the same thing. On March 2, 1955, Claudette Colvin was sixteen years old, a year younger than Darnella Frazier, when she too refused to give her seat to somebody white. She was handcuffed and taken to jail, cursing the police as they led her away.

Word quickly spread that Claudette was pregnant out of wedlock, and E. D. Nixon, Montgomery's most visible Black leader before the emergence of Dr. Martin Luther King, made a difficult decision. He regarded the arrest as a travesty, of course, for he had long been worried about the buses. Not only were they rigidly segregated, with African Americans relegated to seats in the rear, but there was a recurring pattern of cruelty to Black women. Again and again there were reports of female passengers paying their fares then being ordered by the bus driver to go back down the steps and reenter the vehicle from the rear. Even as the women tried to obey, the buses would sometimes drive off without them.

All of this was a reality that Nixon wanted to confront. But he concluded reluctantly that Claudette Colvin was not the right symbol. She was a teenager, after all, and at a vulnerable time in her life, he did not want her subjected to the smears. But nine months later, when the arrest of Rosa Parks triggered the Montgomery bus boycott—a watershed moment in civil rights history—Ms. Colvin would play an important role. As the city's African American community rallied in support of the boycott, and empty buses rumbled through the streets of Montgomery, civil rights attorney Fred Gray filed suit in federal court, demanding desegregation of the buses—seeking to inflict another blow to the whole legal structure of segregation.

Claudette was one of those called to testify.

If her refusal to relinquish her seat the previous March had been an act of spontaneous defiance, her testimony in federal court required a different kind of courage. The unfamiliar grandeur of the setting—the marble courthouse, the judges resplendent in their flowing black robes—called for a measured, clear-headed poise that was not an easy thing for a person so young. But Claudette proved to be a masterful witness.

"I was very hurt," she said. "I didn't know white people would act like that, and I ... I was crying." Every single day, she added, on the city buses of Montgomery, people like herself were "treated wrong, dirty, and nasty."

The emotional force of her testimony (and that of three other African American women) added humanity to the legal theory of the case. The three-judge panel was clearly moved. In a major victory for the civil rights movement, which was then in its fledgling stages, the judges ruled on June 5, 1956: "There is no rational basis upon which the 'separate but equal' doctrine can validly be applied to public transportation in the city of Montgomery."

On December 20, the U.S. Supreme Court agreed. Legal segregation of city buses was unconstitutional. Rosa Parks, understandably, became an icon of the civil rights movement. But the bravery and poise of a teenager, sometimes overlooked in the great sweep of history, were an indisputable part of the story.

Sixty-five years later, as the life and death struggle for equality continued, Darnella Frazier played a similar role. In addition to her initial bravery—mustering the spontaneous courage to withstand the withering stares of Derek Chauvin, even as the life drained out of George Floyd—Darnella was summoned to testify at a trial. Already, of course, her video had sparked some of the largest protests in American history. By one estimate, as many as sixty-five million people had marched against police brutality, and, not at all incidentally, Officer Chauvin was indicted for murder. On March 30, 2021, not quite a year after the killing, Ms. Frazier took the witness stand and wept as she spoke about what she had seen—a man on the ground "scared, terrified, begging for his life. . . . When I look at George Floyd, I look at my dad, I look at my brothers, I look at my cousins, my uncles, because they're all black," she said. "I have a black father. I have a black brother. I have black friends. I look at how that could have been one of them." "It's been nights I stayed up apologizing and apologizing to George Floyd for not doing more and not physically acting and not saving his life. But," she added, as Chauvin sat with his lawyer nearby, "it's like, it's not what I should have done. It's what he should have done."

Partly on the strength of that emotional testimony, Chauvin was convicted of second-degree murder and sentenced to 22.5 years in prison. It was a long sentence—a moment of accountability rare in the annals of police brutality. In our book *The Southernization of America*, coauthor Cynthia Tucker and I tried to put the murder of Mr. Floyd into perspective.

"On the wall of the Equal Justice Initiative's Legacy Museum in Montgomery," we wrote,

> where the goal is to reveal a tapestry of connection between the present and the past, signage notes that in 2015, unarmed black citizens were killed by police at the rate of two a week—a number that mirrored the pace of lynching at its peak. Is this simply a coincidence of history? Perhaps it is. But after the murder of George Floyd, many Americans were confronted by the fact that at the very least his death was not an aberration. The question we all had to answer—and one that remains unanswered—was what exactly we would do about it.

All of us knew that the question was called—rendered unavoidable—by a high school student who did the right thing. As Minnesota governor Tim Walz put it, "Thank God, a young person had a camera . . ."

2.

Emma Gonzalez was also seventeen. And as with Darnella Frazier, we learned about her in a moment of tragedy. She was a junior at Marjorie Stoneman Douglas High School, a suburban school in Parkland, Florida, named for an activist—a feminist-environmentalist who lived to be 108 and, with her book, *River of Grass*, helped save the Everglades. Emma, already, was seen by some of her peers as a rebel. She wore her hair in a buzz cut, which followed a delicate negotiation with her parents. "It's Florida," she said. "Hair is just an extra sweater I'm forced to wear. I even made a PowerPoint presentation to convince my parents to let me shave my head, and it worked."

Whatever the satisfactions of that small victory, there would soon come a time when all such ordinary things would pale. On the afternoon of February 14, 2018, a former student at Stoneman Douglas, Nikolas Cruz, entered Building 12, carrying the mass shooter's weapon of choice, an AR-15-style rifle, designed to kill a lot of people in a hurry. Cruz began a six-minute spree that left fourteen students and three staff members dead.

Emma was in the school auditorium when she heard the alarm. She hid for two hours until police finally gave the all clear. Three days later, with her friend and fellow student, David Hogg, she delivered a speech at the Broward County Courthouse in Fort Lauderdale. On February 20, she and other survivors addressed the state legislature in Tallahassee, and the day after that Gonzalez sparred with a representative of the National Rifle Association at a town hall sponsored by CNN. "You're either funding the killers," she declared, "or you're standing with the children."

But the great moral moment came on March 14 at March for Our Lives—an event she organized with Hogg, Cameron Kasky, and a few other friends. Gazing out across the sea of faces, the thousands who gathered in Washington, D.C., this was the message she delivered through tears:

> Six minutes and about twenty seconds. In a little over six minutes seventeen of our friends were taken from us, fifteen were injured, and everyone, absolutely everyone in the Douglas community, was forever altered. Everyone who was there understands. Everyone who has been touched by the cold grip of gun violence understands. For us, long, tearful, chaotic hours in the scorching afternoon sun were spent not knowing. No one understood the extent of what had happened. No one could believe that there were bodies in that building waiting to be identified for over a day. No one knew that the people who are missing had stopped breathing long before any of us had even known that a code red had been called. No one could comprehend the devastating aftermath or how far this would reach or where this would go.

For those who still can't comprehend because they refuse to, I'll tell you where it went, right into the ground, six feet deep. Six minutes and twenty seconds with an AR-15 and my friend Carmen would never complain to me about piano practice. Aaron Feis would never call Kiera Ms. Sunshine. Alex Schachter would never walk into school with his brother Ryan. Scott Beigel would never joke around with Cameron at camp. Helen Ramsey would never hang out after school with Max. Do you know Montalto would never wave to her friend Liam at lunch? Joaquin Oliver would never play basketball with Sam or Dylan. Alaina Petty would never, Carol Lungren would never, Chris Hixon would never, Luke Hoyer would never, Martin Duque Anguiano would never. Peter Wang would never, Alyssa Alahdeff would never, Jamie Guttenberg would never, Meadow Pollick would never . . .

Now she stood in tight-lipped silence. Tears rolled slowly down her cheeks. Occasionally, she would wipe one away, but she did not make a sound, even as the crowd grew restless, murmuring, a few of them breaking into half-hearted chants, until it occurred to them what she was doing . . . how her silence was a reminder of the crime—of those six excruciating minutes it took for lives to be silenced by a weapon of war . . . a weapon that, when used as intended, could leave a child's body unrecognizable.

Finally, she spoke: "Since the time that I came out here, it has been six minutes and twenty seconds. The shooter has ceased shooting and will soon abandon his rifle. Blend in with the students as they escape and walk free for an hour before arrest. Fight for your lives before it's someone else's job."

There would come a moment when the politicians could not resist, when the ethical force of these young voices required at least some kind of a response. That same month, the Florida legislature passed the Marjorie Stoneman Douglas High School Public Safety Act, which raised the minimum age for buying a gun to twenty-one, expanded background checks, and banned bump stocks, which had made it possible for a mass shooter to fire his weapon even more rapidly.

"You made your voices heard," proclaimed Florida governor Rick Scott.

But darker, more cynical forces awaited. Some would blame the NRA. Others would cite something much broader, some toxic mutation in the culture of guns—and perhaps, in a sense, both understandings were correct. Writing in the *Atlantic*, Ryan Busse, a former gun company executive turned critic of the industry, described a deadly period between 1999 and 2004 when everything changed. Until then, Busse argues, there were at least remnants of moral restraint among industry executives, many of whom supported the ten-year ban on wide-scale production of AR-15s. These were military weapons, after all.

But on April 20, 1999, at Columbine, a suburban high school south of Denver, two teenagers who attended the school went on a killing spree. They murdered twelve classmates and a teacher before turning their weapons on themselves. In one of the great and deadly ironies of history, the National Rifle Association was scheduled to meet the following weekend in Denver. As a gesture of decency, much of that convention was cancelled, but the leaders met behind closed doors. This is Busse's account of what happened next.

> The choice before the NRA, as leaders saw it, was either conciliation and engagement with lawmakers to help draft improved policies or aggressive resistance with the aim of frightening its members into believing lawmakers would come after their guns. The NRA chose to enter the culture-war business, and so did the gun industry.
>
> The Bush administration helped that along by allowing the assault-weapons ban to end in 2004, and, more important, by signing in 2005 the Protection of Lawful Commerce in Arms Act, which shielded the gun industry from liability no matter what kind of irresponsible marketing it used to promote firearms.

And so the floodgates opened. Before Marjorie Stoneman Douglas in Florida, there was Sandy Hook Elementary in Connecticut, where twenty students and six adults died. Afterward, among many others (the number since Columbine is approaching four hundred), one of the most disturbing attacks came at Robb Elementary in Uvalde, Texas, where a gunman with an AR-15 murdered nineteen students and two adults. Police responders cowered outside. They understood correctly that they were outgunned.

Among the Douglas survivors, there was a growing sense that the struggle ahead would be brutal and long. David Hogg, especially, seemed to understand this truth. He enrolled at Harvard, where he continued his involvement with March for Our Lives, making speeches, meeting with legislators, and becoming more discouraged as the death toll mounted. "Objectively, we've failed," he told a writer from *Time* magazine. "I'm not powered by hope. I'm powered by the fact that I have no other choice."

At least for a time, Emma Gonzalez had to let it go. She entered New College, a progressive school in Florida, and found that she was simply overwhelmed—exhausted by the intractability of the struggle, and by a curious celebrity she did not seek. "The pressure almost killed me," she said. And there were other things on her mind. As a student at Marjorie Stoneman Douglas, where she identified as bisexual, she served as head of the Gay-Straight Alliance. At New College, she changed her name to X Gonzalez and her pronoun to "they."

"I should have known for a long time that I don't identify as a girl," they wrote in *New York Magazine*. "I realized then that I'm nonbinary."

In that same article, published in January 2023, Gonzalez returned to the subject of gun violence: "The beat of the mass-shooting metronome is picking up . . . people buy guns every time something scary happens in their community. Something scary is always happening in our communities because people keep buying guns with the intention of using them, and when they use them, it scares more people."

Two months later a shooter armed with AR-15s entered a private Christian school in Nashville and killed three children and three adults. Police arrived quickly, and in contrast to other such events, two young officers, Rex Engelbert and Michael Collazo, though knowing the kind of weapons they would face, rushed the school and killed the shooter within two minutes and fifteen seconds. They said their training "kicked into overdrive."

In the days that followed, thousands of protesters, many of them students in high school and college—a few even younger—descended on the state legislature. On March 30, a group of demonstrators entered the Capitol and occupied the legislative chamber. They were joined by three Democratic legislators, two of whom, Justin Pearson and Justin Jones, carried a bullhorn and led the protesters in chants of "Gun Control Now" and "Power to the People."

After an hour they left—peacefully of their own accord—but House Speaker Cameron Sexton was incensed. As the leader of a Republican supermajority, the Speaker was accustomed to having his way. The Democrats, he said, had "disrupted and dishonored" their legislative body, and he vowed to have them expelled.

On April 2, the legislature voted and Pearson and Jones removed. Gloria Johnson, their legislative colleague who participated in the protest, was not. Pearson and Jones are Black. Johnson is white.

"They hate us," fumed Elie Mystal, an African American writer who serves as justice correspondent for the *Nation*. President Joe Biden called the expelled lawmakers to offer his support.

The national shower of scorn that immediately rained down on Tennessee reminded some of us from another generation of how we felt in Alabama after the Bloody Sunday march. People understood the spite they were seeing on the television screen. So it was again with Tennessee. But the most disconcerting thing for these Republican legislators had to be the dawning realization that they had created new heroes—new symbols of hope—for the gun safety cause.

Justin Pearson, whose neatly trimmed Afro was a visual throwback to the 1960s, was twenty-seven years old (the same age at which Dr. King led the Montgomery Bus Boycott). Pearson was a graduate of Bowdoin College who had grown up in Memphis and possessed a kind of poise and eloquence learned in part from his preacher-father. "You cannot expel our hope," he declared. "You cannot expel our voices. You cannot expel justice."

His colleague, Justin Jones, was a community organizer in Nashville who had played a leading role in removing a bust of Nathan Bedford Forrest, founder of the Ku Klux Klan, from a place of honor at the Tennessee Capitol. Shortly after his expulsion he happened to see Joan Baez as the two of them were passing through the Newark airport. He asked great folksinger, now gray-haired and eighty-two years old, to join him in an impromptu version of "We Shall Overcome"—a song that emerged as a civil rights anthem during the Nashville sit-ins of 1960.

Their rendition, though perhaps a little ragged around the edges, soon went viral on social media. "I'm gonna cry," said Baez when they finished. And Justin Jones touched a hand to his heart.

However inspirational the moment, it also prompted more sober reflection. This was a song, after all, that forever imagined a time in the future, a moment of triumph that had not yet arrived. And Baez, noted one commentator, "still has to sing it."

But there was also this. Justin Pearson and Justin Jones were restored to their legislative seats, reappointed overwhelmingly by the local governments in Nashville and Memphis. Tennessee governor Bill Lee, a Republican, called for new gun safety measures. Lee issued an executive order requiring expanded background checks, and asked the legislature to pass a "red flag law" aimed at keeping guns from the hands of troubled people.

His wife's close friend had died in the shooting.

Before a week had passed, another mass shooter killed six people at a bank in Kentucky. The shooter's mother called 911. Police were unable to respond in time.

We were left with the words of X Gonzalez, written with simple candor and calm: "Treat it like it can happen to you. Because it can."

3.

On a personal note...

There were marchers in multiple cities when Gonzalez delivered her most famous speech. My granddaughter Abby, who was then sixteen, was one of them. She carried a sign that read: "How Loud Do the Screams Have to Be before You Listen?" It was a question filled with frustration and hurt—and no small amount of fear, for the country was descending toward the day when guns would be the leading cause of death among children. But the question implied there must be an answer.

Across the country in Portland, Oregon, my youngest granddaughter Gemma also attended a gun safety rally with her mother. She, too, was filled with dismay and wanted to add her voice to the others. After the Nashville shooting in 2023, I was proud of the fact that at least a thousand of the gun reform marchers came from Vanderbilt University, which is my alma mater. For me they were all, including my granddaughters, the faces of hope—but the faces also of unthinkable possibilities.

We were living in a country where as many twenty million AR-15s—these weapons of war—were in general circulation, and where a member of Congress from my home state introduced legislation to designate this as America's gun. Members of one of our political parties wore its likeness as lapel pins.

My own views on the issues of gun safety and policing had been shaped more than forty years earlier in conversations with a man I admired, Police Chief Ronnie Stone in Charlotte. Chief Stone had worked his way through the ranks from beat cop all the way to the top, and had amassed, I thought, an uncommon amount of street wisdom. Even back then, he was worried about a "hemorrhage" of guns he thought was making the country less safe.

As a reporter for the *Charlotte Observer*, I first interviewed Stone about a Charlotte police officer who had defused a race riot at a local high school. The officer had stepped between two groups of students, one Black, one white, who were armed with chains and two-by-fours and were shouting racial epithets at each other. The policeman, whose name I no longer remember, saw a Frisbee lying on the ground and sailed it at one of the African American students. The student smiled in surprise and sailed it back to the officer, who in turn tossed it to one of the white students. That student tossed it directly to an African American classmate, and soon the threat of racial fighting had morphed into a game of Frisbee.

I asked the officer how he knew to do this. "I just like kids," he replied.

"That's good policing," said Chief Stone.

Around the same time, I had the good fortune to work on a film titled *John and Andy*, produced by Charlotte filmmaker Kathryn Frye, telling the story of two police officers killed in the line of duty. John Burnette and Andy Nobles were heroes—community policemen who worked in one of Charlotte's toughest neighborhoods.

They were killed one night by a robbery suspect who turned a gun on them at point-blank range. The killer hid in a housing project, thinking, apparently, that the "no-snitch" rule would protect him. But the residents knew John and Andy and quickly turned him in. In the days that followed, the stories poured forth. These were young men in their twenties, white guys who had graduated from high school and college, and simply wanted to be cops. Like other community policemen in a city where the crime rate, partly because of their efforts, was dropping, they set out to win the trust of the people. They played basketball with kids in the projects, and coached their teams, and helped organize community watches and cookouts. They pushed landlords to make needed repairs, and visited troubled children in the schools.

But they also made arrests, and were fully aware of the perils of the job. John Burnette once talked to his mother, Trisha Norket, about the possibility that he could be killed. "My brothers and sisters," he said, "will have to get up and go to work the next day. If you are okay, everyone will be okay. Mama, you've got to carry the cue card."

She remembered those words when tragedy struck, and one of the ways she coped with her grief was sharing stories about John and his partners. This was her favorite: Her son, most mornings when he came on duty, would stop to check on an elderly woman who lived in the projects. One day she was having a heart attack, but said she could not go to the hospital because she had been working in her garden and her feet were dirty. Instead of arguing with her, Burnette washed her feet. Then he drove her to the emergency room.

"That's real public service," said Charlotte mayor Richard Vinroot.

His police chief agreed, but also offered an ominous warning. "The guns," he said. There were already too many, making his officers less safe, hardening their fears, making their mission an uphill climb. He was not optimistic about what lay ahead.

Epilogue

In the same month that Justin Jones and Justin Pearson were expelled from the Tennessee legislature, state Representative Zooey Zephyr of Montana was banned from participating in public debate in the legislative chamber of her state after she criticized a bill to deny gender-affirming care passed by the Republican majority. Zephyr, a young transgender woman, said her colleagues would have "blood on their hands"—a reference to the frightful suicide rate among young people who struggle with gender identity without appropriate medical or family support.

Justin Jones was one of the first to rise to her defense, joined by gun safety advocate Maxwell Frost, who in 2023 became the youngest member of the U.S. House of Representatives. Frost proclaimed his own leap of faith. Time, he said, "is not on the side" of the antidemocratic forces.

In this same era, youthful profiles in principle and courage would prove to be bipartisan. On June 28, 2022, Cassidy Hutchinson, who was then twenty-five, testified before the Select Committee to Investigate the January 6 attack on the U.S. Capitol. Hutchinson, who described herself as a conservative Republican, had served as an assistant to President Donald Trump's chief of staff, Mark Meadows. Despite the pressures brought against her at a young age, she offered some of the most compelling testimony against the former president, which she amplified the following year in her best-selling memoir, *Enough*. The people, she said, including the members of her own party, deserved to know the truth.

The Southernization of America

> This excerpt from *The Southernization of America: A Story of Democracy in the Balance*, which I coauthored with Cynthia Tucker, was published in the *Guardian*. The book was published by NewSouth Books in Montgomery, now an imprint of the University of Georgia Press.

In 1974, the great Southern journalist John Egerton wrote a prescient book titled *The Americanization of Dixie: The Southernization of America*. In a series of connected but self-contained essays, he made the point that something fundamental was changing—both in his native South, and in the country as a whole. But even Egerton seemed not to be sure exactly how things would unfold.

He was, as those of us who knew him could attest, one of the great and gentle souls of his time, a man deeply committed to racial justice who wanted badly to believe that it would be a good thing if this troubled place in which he lived—this part of America that had once fought a war for the right to own slaves—could emerge from the strife of the civil rights years somehow chastened and wiser for the journey, if it could narrow its distance from the rest of the country and perhaps even lead it toward better days. That was the hope. But Egerton, as was his habit, saw darker possibilities as well. Giving voice to his fears, he wrote, "The South and the nation are not exchanging strengths as much as they are exchanging sins; more often than not, they are sharing and spreading the worst in each other, while the best languishes and withers."

For a while it was easy enough to make the case that Egerton's gloom was misplaced, or at least overstated. The anecdotal evidence was all around. In Virginia, Republican governor Linwood Holton had stunned political observers when he was elected in 1969 on a promise of racial reconciliation. In contrast to the Southern Democrats who had controlled Virginia for a hundred years, Holton proclaimed that the "era of defiance"—of resistance to civil rights progress—was coming to an end. He supported school desegregation, appointed women and minorities to state government, and promised to make Virginia "a model in race relations." In Florida, new Democratic governor Reubin Askew sounded nearly identical themes. He supported busing as a tool for integrating schools—a moral and educational imperative, he said—and while appointing African Americans to the highest levels of state government, he set such a standard for integrity and competence that Harvard's John F. Kennedy School of Government rated him one of the top ten governors of the twentieth century. And, of course, there was Jimmy Carter. Elected governor of Georgia in 1970, Carter proclaimed in his inaugural address that "the time for racial discrimination is over." Easily the most ambitious of these New South champions, he soon set out for the presidency with Southernness at the heart of his appeal:

> I've been the product of an emerging South. I see the clear advantages of throwing off the millstone of racial prejudice. I think it's a process that's compatible with the moral and ethical standards of our nation—the heritage of our country, as envisioned by our forefathers. I also see that we have a special responsibility here. When we are meek, or quiescent, or silent on the subject of civil rights at home or human rights abroad, there is no other voice on Earth that can replace the lost voice, the absent voice, of the United States. This is what the persecutors want, and this is what the persecuted fear.

For many Americans, it was mesmerizing—a peanut farmer from the deepest South reconnecting the country with its finest ideals. In 1976, when Carter won the Democratic nomination, he stood side by side at the national convention, gazing out across the sea of delegates, with Martin Luther King Sr. There they were, two native Georgians, one Black, one white, a Southern governor and a civil rights lion, sharing a moment that felt like a revival—not only of the faith they both proclaimed but of a dream deferred—of shining hopes and possibilities in which so many of us wanted to believe.

"Surely the Lord," shouted Daddy King over the mad cacophony of music and cheers amid descending balloons, "is in this place."

There was intoxication in the moment, but we knew it was shadowed by something very different—the realities John Egerton was writing about. In the presidential election of 1968, Richard Nixon had embarked on a Southern strategy, and he did not mean the things that Jimmy Carter was telling us. In a sense, Nixon's mentor had been George Wallace. He watched in private admiration as the Alabama governor, who had pledged in 1963 his commitment to "segregation forever," learned to redefine his appeal. In the presidential primaries of 1964 and 1968, Wallace spoke more obliquely about race, almost as if he were teaching the nation how to think in code.

From the time he famously stood in the schoolhouse door, he had begun to polish that skill. Everybody understood in the summer of 1963 the mission at hand, how Wallace was embarked on a doomed, quixotic quest to block the admission of Black students Vivian Malone and James Hood to the University of Alabama. But just as secessionists a hundred years earlier had talked about states' rights when they really meant slavery, Wallace cast the federal government as a bully—an outside force pursuing integration without regard for the will of the people—and himself as a noble defender of freedom. A few years later, on the campaign trail for the presidency, he found it useful not to mention segregation but to talk about "liberal sob sisters," or "bleeding heart sociologists," or "some bearded Washington bureaucrat who can't even park a bicycle straight."

All the shared resentments were there, but he and his audience felt shielded from the charge—his accusers frustrated as they attempted to make it—that they were bigots at heart. There were times when he couldn't contain himself. Once in 1968 he invoked the specter of urban riots—those moments when African American rage, often in response to police brutality, erupted into violence became, in a sense, a magnified reflection of the crime.

"We don't have riots down in Alabama," Wallace roared, bantamweight defiance flashing in his eyes. "They start a riot down there, first one of 'em to pick up a brick gets a bullet to the brain. And then you walk over to the next one and say, 'All right, pick up a brick. We just want to see you pick up one of them bricks, now!'"

Newsman Douglas Kiker of NBC, observing the response of a Midwestern crowd, was struck by a sudden, horrifying epiphany: "They all hate black people, all of them. They're all afraid . . . Great God! That's it! They're all Southern! The whole United States is Southern!"

There were African American activists, people such as James Baldwin or Malcolm X, who begged to differ. Both had written with urgency about the indigenous racism of the North. But if the story was more complicated, if racism had already taken root in every nook and corner of America, was there nevertheless something in Kiker's moment of revelation? In this era of homogenization, when television and interstate highways—and soon enough, the Internet—were erasing the isolation of the South, pulling it into the national mainstream, was there something about our place that was beginning to reshape the country? And if there was, might it be a source of mystical promise? Or was it, more inevitably, a reality overflowing with dread?

Ever since colonial times, the South, with its reliance on slavery as the backbone for its economy, has been the epicenter for American racism. As Alexander Stephens, vice president of the Confederacy, said of his new secessionist state, "Its cornerstone rests upon the great truth that the negro is not equal to the white man."

In her runaway bestseller *Caste*, Isabel Wilkerson makes the case that this assumption, sometimes less venomously stated, never really disappeared from the American psyche and began, in fact, to make a comeback in 2008. Two things happened that year. First, the U.S. Census Bureau issued a prediction that by 2042—not that far in the future—whites would no longer make up a majority of Americans—a plurality, yes, but no longer a majority capable of imposing its will. And then, as if to illustrate the possibility, a Black man was elected president.

"I went to bed last night," lamented Rush Limbaugh, after Obama was reelected in 2012, "thinking we're outnumbered. I went to bed last night thinking we've lost the country. I don't know how else you look at this."

As Wilkerson noted, the fears that Limbaugh put into words led to measures more concrete than a pundit's bombast. As Tea Party Republicans vowed to "take our country back," the GOP began changing election laws, making it harder to vote. Only two years before Obama's election, President Bush had signed an extension of the Voting Rights Act that passed overwhelmingly in the U.S. House of Representatives and unanimously in the U.S. Senate. The right to vote was a bipartisan truth, touted by a Republican president as one of his cornerstone commitments. But no longer. On June 25, 2013, in a case coming out of Alabama, the U.S. Supreme Court gutted key provisions of the Voting Rights Act, and in the next three years nearly sixteen million people were deleted from voter registration lists.

Meanwhile, there was hatred in the air. Social media posts compared the president and First Lady to monkeys and apes, armed participants at political rallies carried signs proclaiming "Death to Obama"; and one day during the birther controversy, a man parked his car on Constitution Avenue and began firing his semiautomatic rifle toward the upper floors of the White House—toward the rooms where the First Family lived. A bullet lodged in the windowsill. (The shooter is in federal prison, slated to be released in 2033.)

But perhaps most ominously, as a measure of the free-floating rage, by 2015 police were killing unarmed African Americans at five times the rate of whites—at a rate that was a disturbing reminder of the rate of lynching in the Jim Crow era. Two years later, during the Trump administration, children of color were being seized and separated from their parents in an effort to deter illegal immigration, and that, too, for many of us raised with the shame of Southern history, was an echo of the past.

On a quiet downtown street in Montgomery, Alabama, an old warehouse with a long, dark history, stands now as a memorial—a museum that opened in 2018, created by the Equal Justice Initiative to trace the through line running from slavery to the present day, from the terrorism of lynching and the humiliations of racial segregation to a criminal justice system that, among other things, creates a climate for police brutality. As soon as you walk through the door, you see on the wall the words of a man held captive here, recounting a particular moment of horror: "I saw a mother lead seven children to the auction block. She knew some of them would be taken from her; but they took all. The children were sold to a slave trader. I met that mother in the street, and her wild, haggard face lives in my mind today. She wrung her hands in anguish and exclaimed, 'Gone, all gone! Why don't God kill me?'"

Preserving such history is one major purpose of the EJI. Bryan Stevenson, the organization's founder, is a lawyer who spends much of his time working through a legal system he knows is flawed, opposing capital punishment and other harsh sentences imposed upon people on the margins of American life. But Stevenson also believes the nation must remember and reckon with the past—and because we have never mustered the will, we hear its echoes even now. There are few echoes more stark or elemental than the cries of children taken from their parents.

Steve Schmidt, former campaign strategist for John McCain, worries that under the leadership of Donald Trump, the party in which he believed began moving not toward a reckoning but resolutely in the opposite direction, stirring the ancient hatreds of race.

But there was another side to the story, also emanating from the South. In Atlanta, which had emerged first as a center of African American education, and then, not at all coincidentally, as the epicenter of the Southern civil rights movement, younger activists such as Stacey Abrams heeded the call of movement icon John Lewis.

"Ordinary people with extraordinary vision," Lewis wrote near the end of his life, "can redeem the soul of America by getting in what I call good trouble, necessary trouble. Voting and participating in the democratic process are key. The vote is the most powerful nonviolent change agent you have in a democratic society. You must use it because it is not guaranteed. You can lose it."

By autumn 2020, Abrams and others led a vigorous network of voter advocacy groups working to turn out a multiracial coalition in Georgia. The far-reaching effort worked. Joe Biden won Georgia, and was the first Democrat to win the presidential contest in the state since Bill Clinton's first run in 1992. Georgia also elected Raphael Warnock, pastor of Ebenezer Baptist Church, once the home pulpit of Dr. Martin Luther King Jr., as the first African American to represent Georgia in the U.S. Senate.

In his maiden speech to that body, Warnock offered this assessment of the election—and of the state of things in America:

> I am a proud son of the great state of Georgia.... At the time of my birth, Georgia's two senators were Richard B. Russell and Herman E. Talmadge, both arch segregationists and unabashed adversaries of the civil rights movement. After the Supreme Court's landmark Brown v. Board ruling, outlawing school segregation, Talmadge warned that "blood will run in the streets of Atlanta."... Yet there is something in the American covenant, in its charter documents and Jeffersonian ideals that bends toward freedom. And led by a preacher and a patriot named King, Americans of all races stood up. History vindicated the movement that sought to bring us closer to our ideals, to lengthen and strengthen the cords of democracy. And I now hold the seat, the Senate seat, where Herman E. Talmadge sat. And that's why I love America...

All of this, he said, was the heart of the promise springing from his place. But there was another dimension to the story, an emerging threat to the foundations of democracy, spreading, like the progress he had seen in his life, from Georgia to every corner of the country: "The people of Georgia sent their first African American senator—and first Jewish senator, my brother, Jon Ossoff—to these hallowed halls. But then what happened? . . . We are witnessing right now a massive and unabashed assault on voting rights and voter access unlike anything we have seen since the Jim Crow era. . . . And the question before all of us at every moment is, what will we do?"

This, he said, is the cold reality of our time. If it is true, as John Egerton has written, that the South and the nation have exchanged sins, Warnock holds out the hope that we might somehow exchange virtues as well. But time is running short, and American democracy hangs in the balance.

Keeper of the Faith

> This reflection on the life of the Reverend Steve Dill, originally a Facebook post, was expanded slightly and published by *UM News/United Methodist Communications* on January 28, 2022.

My friend Steve Dill died the other day. He was ninety-three with a failing heart, so this was not entirely unexpected, but it is to me sadder than I have words to express. I am not alone in this. Steve was a United Methodist minister who embodied the faith as I understand it . . . as a mystical presence; a source of mystery at least as much as it was of pious truth. He was ninety when he preached the eulogy for my wife Nancy—white haired, ramrod straight, with a voice that had to remind you of God's. On that occasion, he said, "When Nancy died, it was as if she ceased to meet us in a particular place in order to meet us everywhere."

I found myself thinking of the first time Nancy and I heard Steve preach. At its Emancipation Day service, an African American church in Mobile asked him to deliver the white apology for slavery. For his sermon text, Steve chose the old Negro hymn "Were You There When They Crucified My Lord?" Of course none of us was physically present for the crucifixion, just as none of us was alive to own slaves. But Steve quoted the hymn's refrain: "Sometimes it causes me to tremble." As he recounted the racial history of the country—a brilliant summary of the great American sin—he paused periodically to reaffirm, "Sometimes it causes me to tremble." Nancy leaned over to me and whispered, "You have to collect his sermons into a book, and you have to make sure it gets published." So I did.

In that book *The Poetry of Faith: Sermons Preached in a Southern Church*, I wrote an introduction about Steve's life—how his ministry was forged in the civil rights years when he stood for social justice and spoke against racial segregation. He did this in Alabama in the 1960s, when it was not easy. But there was something else about him in those days. As his fellow minister Gorman Houston put it, "Steve never lost himself in the battle. That was what was so remarkable. He never distanced himself from the people he disagreed with. He had a pastoral way, never letting go of his strong stands, but also never letting go of his kindness."

To which I added,

> Almost invariably, the poetry of his preaching caught the quick of my imagination and quietly, inevitably made me think. . . . In saying this, I speak as a skeptic, as one afflicted by the shadow of doubt, but even more so as a reluctant critic of American Christianity—of the didactic shrillness emanating from so many of our pulpits. . . . You won't find any of that from Steve Dill, nothing harsh, or narrow, or petty; nothing simplistic or disingenuous. Instead what you'll discover is a rigorous mind in search of deeper truth, and a faith in the loving mysteries of God.

Now we come to the moment of his passing. The human family is poorer, less compassionate and wise, than it was with Steve in it. But there is gratitude, too, as we muster the grace to remember who he was. In a wrenchingly beautiful eulogy delivered at the funeral, Houston noted that in the case of Steve Dill, it really did seem as if the word became flesh.

That's a metaphor, of course; all too often an empty cliché spoken by people who mean something different from what Gorman understood or from the life Steve lived. As Gorman explained, Dill embodied all of those qualities—the eloquence, the kindness, the curious mind, the commitment to justice and reconciliation, the *faith*—that could make the world better if we would only allow it. Many of us, I think, left the church that day filled with sadness—but also with a flickering hope that defied the reality of our time.

Musings
Commencement 2018

> One of the singular honors of my career was working for the University of South Alabama during the presidency of the late Tony Waldrop. I thought he led with intelligence and heart. For sure, he supported my work, the writing, the teaching, and the public programs, which very often pushed against the grain of popular opinion in Alabama. In 2018, Dr. Waldrop asked me to deliver the commencement address at South Alabama's graduation. I was grateful. It seemed like a good opportunity to reflect upon the state of the country.

We come together today in a time of celebration. All of you in this room have achieved something extraordinary. You have earned your college degree with all of the possibilities that it will open up in your lives.

None of us should denigrate our fellow citizens who work hard every day without such a degree. Nearly all of them do valuable work—often really hard work—that is important to their families and to the functioning of our society. But more and more, theirs is an uphill path.

With your degree, you have improved exponentially the possibility that you can build a satisfying—and prosperous—career for yourselves and for your families.

There is a good chance that roughly half of you in this graduating class are the first in your families to achieve this impressive milestone. That must carry with it an even greater sense of satisfaction—and almost certainly of gratitude for the support you have received along the way. Speaking for every faculty and family member in this room, we are proud of you. But if this is a moment of celebration, the time may come—and it may come soon—when it is also a moment of sober reflection. You will soon go forth not only as credentialed members of the workforce but also as citizens of a troubled world. You may or may not wish to think of it that way. But you are very likely to discover that you have no choice.

Fifty years ago this month, I found myself in the place where you are now, having completed my undergraduate degree—with a fairly unimpressive grade point average, but in my case, with a burning desire to write about the problems affecting our country.

And the problems seemed massive.

I want to talk briefly about those times—and the perspective I think they offer for today. America in 1968 was, as it is again today, a deeply divided land. And there were—inexplicably as we see today—national leaders who were seeking to make those divisions worse, to govern the country by appealing to our fears.

And there was plenty of reason to fear. There were assassinations, riots in our inner cities, an unpopular war in Vietnam that divided the people of my generation and others.

But there were also, as there are today, people about your age working as hard and as passionately as they knew how, in order to change realities that seemed unjust, or seemed to be a threat to the common good.

Beginning in 1960, and continuing for a number of years after that, there were young African American students—often dressed in their Sunday finest—sitting in at restaurants that refused them service simply because of the color of their skin.

In 1964 and 1965, young people Black and white came to Mississippi or marched across the Edmund Pettus Bridge in Selma so that every citizen would have a right to vote. There were women, young and old, who demanded equal pay for equal work, and were inspired, in part, by the recent invention of the birth control pill to demand the right to control their own bodies. There were people planning the first Earth Day in pursuit of a sustainable planet for all of us to live on. And there were Mexican American farmworkers in California, and African American sanitation workers in Memphis, led by Dr. Martin Luther King on the very eve of his assassination, demanding better pay and safer conditions for their work, raising broader concerns of economic justice.

Our brothers and sisters who were gay demanded that their rights be respected.

Those of us who supported these causes really believed that we could make a great country greater—one that embodied more fully its founding ideals that all of us are created equal: not in our abilities, of course, but in the eyes of the law, and in the basic rights that come with being an American—life and liberty and the pursuit of happiness—the opportunity to chase our own dreams.

And many of us also believed in the religious ideals on which we were raised, that we were all children of God and therefore brothers and sisters of one another.

We believed we could build a country where all of this was true, where all these ideals would be more fully realized than they had ever been before. And of course we failed.

I don't mean to say that we failed completely. During those years a Democratic president with the bipartisan support of Congress passed the Civil Rights Act of 1964, ending legal segregation, and the Voting Rights Act of 1965, which created a multiracial democracy in the American South, where it had not existed before. Those are no small things. And a Republican president, also with bipartisan support, established the Environmental Protection Agency to help preserve the health of our planet.

But to understand the degree to which we came up short, all you have to do is look around at the problems that still confront us today.

Scientists commissioned by the United Nations tell us that we have twelve years—*twelve*—to reverse the reality of global warming before it's irrevocably too late, and the killer hurricanes and California wildfires will pale beside the effects of coastal flooding that might well destroy some of the world's most important cities.

At the same time, global poverty and regional wars have become so widespread that great human migrations—people who are desperately trying to survive—can threaten the stability of countries affected less directly.

Our own nation has always been a place where desperate people could come. But is it still? And if so, how do we deal with that responsibility?

Income inequality, a deadly reality throughout human history from the Roman Empire to the Russian Revolution, is becoming worse in our own country.

And then there is violence—the horrifying mass shootings in our schools, violence against women and people who are gay, gang violence spreading terror on the streets of our cities, and, all too often, violence against people of color committed by police.

And we seem to be so deeply divided that we are paralyzed in the face of these realities. I'm not here today to propose a new set of policies or specific solutions for these and other problems. I am not even sure I know what those policies should be. But what I will submit to you today is that we will, somehow, have to find a way to do better, and your generation will have to lead us in that effort.

And so I want to offer a word of caution.

I remember at the time of my own graduation, which was, as I have said, also a time of great division, many of us were so sure we were right that we simply tried to outshout the people who disagreed. I did this myself until, in 1971, I read an article in *Harper's* magazine by the great American journalist Bill Moyers, titled "Listening to America." What Moyers was saying in that article was that our self-indulgent national divisions were tearing away "the veneer of civility" that allows a fragile democracy to function. And the only antidote to that was to learn once again how to listen to each other.

I've thought a lot recently about that article, and about the warnings and encouragement of other social commentators writing today. In Jon Meacham's new book *The Soul of America: The Battle for Our Better Angels* and Doris Kearns Goodwin's *Leadership in Turbulent Times*, we are reminded what can happen in this country if we reach for the best that is in us instead of the worst—and if we demand that our leaders do the same.

It has always been the great frontier of the human experience—perhaps our most difficult challenge—to live in peace and mutual respect with people who are not exactly like we are. There may be differences in political philosophy, or in the color of our skins, or in the name we give to the god of our prayers. But what writers like Meacham, Moyers, and Goodwin are telling us is that we live in a land where we can—and must—find a way to cross these barriers and heal our divisions.

We have done it before, and therefore, certainly, we can do it again. Otherwise, our future is not bright.

We all know that this is true, don't we? The truth of the danger and the truth of the hope. All of us have encountered the decency and good will of people who are different—of people with whom we disagree. And so I would submit to you today that the time has come to relearn the art of creative disagreement—to find a path toward honest dialogue in confronting the problems of our country and the world. We have got to learn once again to listen.

I want to end by saying that I am certain you can do this. I am even more certain that we all have to try. So I urge you to go forth with confidence from this moment of celebration, of pride and satisfaction in what you have achieved, and what that achievement portends for the future. Good luck on the journey that lies ahead.

And now enjoy the rest of your day. Give yourselves a round of applause. You have earned it.

ACKNOWLEDGMENTS

Special thanks to Cynthia Tappan, Sue Walker, Cynthia Tucker, Kent Rush, and my late friend, Peter Cooper, for their support of this project. I'm grateful to Candice Fairchild for her illustration and early work as an editor on the manuscript, and to Kim Graves and Debbie Outlaw for their logistical help in transforming a pile of published articles into an intelligible manuscript. I will remain forever grateful for my eighteen years as writer in residence at the University of South Alabama, and especially to my colleagues Steve Trout, Ellen Harrington, Charlotte Pence, Andrzej Wierzbicki, David Johnson, Becky McLaughlin, Susan Santoli, Andi Kent, Kern Jackson, Justine Burbank, and the late Tony Waldrop for their belief and encouragement in my creative efforts.

ABOUT THE AUTHOR

Frye Gaillard, former writer in residence at the University of South Alabama, is the author of more than thirty books, including such award-winning titles as *A Hard Rain: America in the 1960s; Cradle of Freedom: Alabama and the Movement That Changed America; The Southernization of America: A Story of Democracy in the Balance* (coauthored with Cynthia Tucker); and *Watermelon Wine: The Spirit of Country Music*. In 2025, Gaillard was inducted into the Alabama Writers Hall of Fame.